Classroom **Testing** and **Assessment** for **ALL** Students

Classroom **Testing** and **Assessment** for **ALL** Students

Beyond Standardization

SPENCER J. SALEND

CORWIN
A SAGE Company

For information:

Corwin
A SAGE Company
2455 Teller Road
Thousand Oaks, California 91320
(800) 233-9936
Fax: (800) 417-2466
www.corwinpress.com

SAGE India Pvt. Ltd.
B 1/I 1 Mohan Cooperative
  Industrial Area
Mathura Road, New Delhi
India 110 044

SAGE Ltd.
1 Oliver's Yard
55 City Road
London EC1Y 1SP
United Kingdom

SAGE Asia-Pacific Pte. Ltd.
33 Pekin Street #02-01
Far East Square
Singapore 048763

Printed in the United States of America.

Library of Congress Cataloging-in-Publication Data

Salend, Spencer J.
Classroom testing and assessment for all students: Beyond standardization/Spencer J. Salend.
    p. cm.
Includes bibliographical references and index.
ISBN 978-1-4129-6642-9 (cloth)
ISBN 978-1-4129-6643-6 (pbk.)
    1. Educational tests and measurements—United States. 2. Test-taking skills—Study and teaching—United States. I. Title.

LB3051.S242 2009
371.27'1—dc22   2009019900

This book is printed on acid-free paper.

09   10   11   12   13   10 9 8 7 6 5 4 3 2 1

Acquisitions Editor:	David Chao
Editorial Assistant:	Brynn Saito
Production Editor:	Libby Larson
Copy Editor:	Claire Larson
Typesetter:	C&M Digitals (P) Ltd.
Proofreader:	Theresa Kay
Indexer:	Terri Corry
Cover Designer:	Karine Hovsepian

Contents

Acknowledgments

I would like to thank my colleagues at Corwin: David Chao, Libby Larson, Brynn Saito, and Allyson Sharp. I appreciate their commitment to quality, diversity, and collaboration and their dedication to the field. I truly value their support, guidance, and friendship. My appreciation also goes to Claire Larson for her invaluable assistance in copy editing the book. Finally, I also want to acknowledge my students and colleagues.

PUBLISHER'S ACKNOWLEDGMENTS

Corwin gratefully acknowledges the contributions of the following individuals:

Kathryn Amacher
Special Education Teacher
Franklin Middle School
Wheaton, IL

Erin E. Barton
Assistant Professor
University of Oregon
Eugene, OR

Janette Bowen
Teacher (6th Grade CWC/SPED)
Junction City Middle School
Junction City, KS

Phyllis N. Levert
College Professor
Kennesaw State University
Marietta, GA

Amy McCart
Research Assistant Professor
University of Kansas
Lawrence, KS

Mary McGriff
Former Elementary School Principal; Graduate Assistant
Rutgers University Graduate School of Education
New Brunswick, NJ

Jelisa Coltrane Wolfe
Director of Special Education
Staunton City Schools
Staunton, VA

About the Author

Photo by Emi DiSciullo

A former teacher in the New York City school system, Spencer J. Salend is a professor at State University of New York at New Paltz, where he teaches courses on educational assessment and serves as the coordinator of the special education program. He is the author of the best-selling, easy-to-read, and practical book, *Creating Inclusive Classrooms: Effective and Reflective Practices* (2008). Widely known for his work in translating research into practice, he has published and presented on such topics as educational assessment, inclusive educational practices, and students from culturally and linguistically diverse backgrounds. In recognition of the significance of his research and its benefits to others, he was selected as a recipient of the State University of New York's Faculty Scholar Award and the Chancellor's Research Recognition Award. He has also served as a project director and program evaluator for numerous federal and state projects and has shared his work by engaging in a variety of professional development and activities.

To Suzanne, Jack, and Madison. You send me.

Introducing Inclusive Classroom Testing and Assessment Practices

As part of the districtwide curriculum related to the study of the solar system, Ms. Rodriguez's class worked on a unit about the sun, the moon, and the planets that was aligned to statewide learning standards. Before implementing the unit, Ms. Rodriguez and her teaching team collaborated to plan it and agreed upon the curricular goals that students should achieve. The team members discussed how they would measure their students' learning and decided to use a test and a menu of various performance assessment activities linked to their instructional goals.

The team created a test that included a variety of objective and essay questions related to the solar system, which would be given to students at the end of the instructional unit. To make their test more motivating and readable, they paired visuals such as pictorials of the planets, the moon, and the sun with texts. To help students prepare for the test, Ms. Rodriguez gave them a study guide outlining important information about the content and format of the test. Ms. Rodriguez also conducted a review of key topics and vocabulary from the unit by having students play a game using active responding clickers and an interactive whiteboard. Ms. Rodriguez used the students' responses to identify those students who needed additional instruction to learn important concepts and terminology. On the day of the test, Ms. Rodriguez gave all of her students the option of taking the test on a computer. Some of her students received the testing accommodations outlined in their individualized educational programs (IEPs).

In addition to the test, Ms. Rodriguez used classroom assessments to document her students' learning. She prepared a menu of performance assessment activities that included posting a Web page, giving a PowerPoint or Keynote presentation, writing a blog or a wiki, and creating a podcast or a digital video about the unique characteristics of the sun, the moon, or a planet. Ms. Rodriguez and her students reviewed the menu before all students chose strategies from the list for sharing their learning. Ms. Rodriguez kept a record of students' choices and encouraged them to try new activities throughout the school year.

At the end of the instructional unit, Ms. Rodriguez and her colleagues met to examine students' tests and learning products to identify students who had mastered the unit's instructional goals as well as those who needed additional or modified instruction. They also used this information to reflect on the effectiveness of the instructional strategies they used and the ways they could improve their teaching.

Through the experiences of Ms. Rodriguez and the other teachers you will read about throughout this book, you will examine best practices for implementing inclusive classroom testing and assessments that support your students' learning and inform your teaching. *Inclusive classroom testing and assessment practices* involve tailoring your teacher-made tests and assessments to the individual strengths and challenges of your students by examining and varying the following:

- *Content* that will be the focus of your classroom tests and assessments
- *Process* you will use to create and administer your teacher-made tests and to conduct classroom assessments
- *Tests and learning products* your students will complete to demonstrate and display their learning
- *Motivational techniques* you will use to prompt and encourage your students to perform at their optimal level on your classroom tests and assessments
- *Classroom and testing environmental features* that you will use to support and enhance student performance (Price & Nelson, 2007).

ELEMENTS OF INCLUSIVE CLASSROOM TESTING AND ASSESSMENT PRACTICES

As you read this book, consider the following elements of inclusive classroom testing and assessment practices, which can guide you in implementing the best practices presented in each chapter.

Element: Inclusive classroom testing and assessment practices are appropriate for use with all students (Salend, 2008; Tomlinson, 2008). Inclusive classroom testing and assessment practices can be used to accommodate not only the varied academic, cognitive, language, social, behavioral, and technological skill levels of your students, but also their cultural, linguistic, and experiential backgrounds. These best practices are designed to help *all* of your students access and succeed on your classroom tests and assessments. Their implementation should support and have minimal or no impact on the curriculum mastery expectations you have for your students, your teaching, and the structure or content of your educational program.

Element: Inclusive classroom testing and assessment practices incorporate the principles of universal design for learning (UDL; Kurtts, Matthews, & Smallwood, 2009; Sopko, 2008). Incorporating the principles of UDL into your classroom tests and assessments can foster your development and implementation of flexible testing and assessment materials and strategies that are appropriate and accessible to *all* of your students (Sopko, 2008). These principles, which are presented in Figure 1, offer options that allow you to plan and implement your testing and assessment practices so that they are inclusive of *all* your students by providing the following:

- *Multiple means of representation,* by which you present your testing and assessment materials in varied ways so that *all* students can access and understand them. For instance, Ms. Rodriguez designed text and used graphics, symbols, and highlighting to make her test more motivating and readable so her students could understand her test's directions (see Chapter 1).
- *Multiple means of expression,* by which you offer your students a variety of ways to demonstrate their learning. For instance, just as Ms. Rodriguez did at the beginning of this introduction, you can allow your students to choose a way to showcase their learning from a menu of classroom assessment activities that you have presented to them (see Chapter 5). Also, like Ms. Rodriguez, you can provide your students with the testing accommodations they need to respond to test items (see Chapter 2) and offer them the option of taking tests via technology (see Chapter 3).

- *Multiple means of engagement*, by which you use classroom testing and assessment practices that prompt, motivate, and encourage students to perform at their optimal levels. Like Ms. Rodriguez, you can guide them in making choices about how to demonstrate their learning and help them develop the study and test-taking skills they need to succeed on your tests (see Chapter 4).

Figure 0.1   The Principles of Universal Design for Learning and Inclusive Classroom Testing and Assessment Practices

Universal Design for Learning Principles	Universal Design for Learning Principles and Inclusive Classroom Testing and Assessment Practices	Examples of the Implementation of Universal Design Principles and Inclusive Classroom Testing and Assessment Practices
Principle 1: Equitable use	Testing and assessment materials, strategies, and environments are designed so that they are useful, appealing, and safe for all students to use. They are respectful of individual differences and are used by all students in similar or equivalent ways and in different contexts.	• Create valid and accessible tests (see Chapter 1) • Provide all students with valid and appropriate testing accommodations (see Chapter 2)
Principle 2: Flexible use	Testing and assessment materials, strategies, and environments are designed so that they accommodate the individual preferences and abilities of all students. They are flexible in providing choices in terms of the methods and pace of use.	• Allow students to take technology-based tests (see Chapter 3) • Use a range of classroom-based assessment practices (see Chapter 5)
Principle 3: Simple and intuitive use	Testing and assessment materials, strategies, and environments are designed so that they are easy for all students to use and understand. Their use is not dependent on students' experiences, prior knowledge, language and literacy skills, and other learning preferences and abilities.	• Make sure the test's directions are clearly presented and that test items are formatted appropriately (see Chapter 1) • Administer tests via technology (see Chapter 3)
Principle 4: Perceptible information	Testing and assessment materials, strategies, and environments are designed so that they communicate essential information to all students. They present critical information to all students using multiple formats, backgrounds with sufficient contrasts, legible text guidelines, and compatible teaching, testing and assessment techniques, and assistive technology devices.	• Enhance the readability and legibility of testing materials (see Chapter 1) • Use a variety of classroom-based assessment techniques (see Chapter 5) • Develop and administer tests using technology (see Chapters 1 and 3)

(Continued)

Figure 0.1 (Continued)

Universal Design for Learning Principles	Universal Design for Learning Principles and Inclusive Classroom Testing and Assessment Practices	Examples of the Implementation of Universal Design Principles and Inclusive Classroom Testing and Assessment Practices
Principle 5: Tolerance for error	Testing and assessment materials, strategies, and environments are designed to minimize errors, adverse consequences, and unintentional actions. They provide safeguards and warnings to assist all students in using them safely and efficiently.	• Teach students to use effective study and test-taking skills and strategies (see Chapter 4) • Embed feedback, motivation, and error minimization into tests (see Chapters 1 and 3) • Provide students with valid and appropriate testing accommodations (see Chapter 2) • Use effective guidelines for creating test questions (see Chapter 1)
Principle 6: Low physical effort	Testing and assessment materials, strategies, and environments are designed to be used comfortably and without much physical effort by all students. They allow all students to use them with a range of reasonable physical actions, and do not require repetitive actions or sustained physical effort.	• Provide students with the technology and testing accommodations they need to take tests (see Chapters 2 and 3) • Teach students to use effective study and test-taking skills and strategies (see Chapter 4)
Principle 7: Size and space approach and use	Testing and assessment materials, strategies and environments are designed for use by all students regardless of their body size, posture, and mobility. They allow all students to see, reach, and activate important features and information and offer sufficient space for assistive technology devices and personal assistance.	• Provide students with the technology and testing accommodations they need to take tests (see Chapters 2 and 3) • Format tests appropriately (see Chapter 1)
Principle 8: Community of learners	Testing and assessment materials, strategies, and environments promote socialization and communication for all students.	• Have students work in groups to study for and take tests (see Chapters 2 and 4) • Have students work in collaborative groups to complete a range of classroom assessment practices (see Chapter 5)
Principle 9: Inclusive environment	Testing and assessment materials, strategies, and environments foster acceptance and a sense of belonging for all students.	• Have students work in collaborative groups to take tests and complete a range of classroom assessment practices (see Chapters 2 and 5) • Use inclusive classroom testing and assessment practices with all students (see Chapters 1 through 5)

Source: McGuire, Scott, & Shaw, 2006; Salend, 2008; Sopko, 2008.

Because there is overlap among the UDL principles, many of the examples of their implementation presented in Figure 0.1 can used to address multiple principles.

Element: Inclusive classroom testing and assessment practices can be supported by the use of technology (Boone & Higgins, 2007; Ketterlin-Geller, Yovanoff, & Tindal, 2007; King-Sears & Evmenova, 2007; Thompson, Quenemoen, & Thurlow, 2006). Technology can be an excellent way to incorporate the principles of UDL into your classroom testing and assessments. As you will see in this book (especially Chapters 3 and 5), you can use a range of low and high assistive and instructional technologies to implement the best practices presented in each chapter. Whereas *assistive technologies* such as augmentative communication systems and screen magnification programs are used by your students to increase, maintain, or improve their functional capabilities, *instructional technologies* such as interactive whiteboards (e.g., SMART Boards), clickers, blogs, and PowerPoint presentations are used by you and your students to facilitate the teaching and learning processes. *Low-tech* refers to devices that are usually inexpensive, nonelectric, readily available, homemade, and easy for students and teachers to learn to use, such as line guides, reading rulers, and index cards used to assist students who have difficulty tracking and maintaining their place when reading a line of text. *High-tech* relates to devices that tend to be electronic, commercially produced, relatively expensive, and require some training to use, such as word processing and voice recognition systems.

Element: Inclusive classroom testing and assessment practices address both formative and summative assessment (Chappuis & Chappuis, 2008; Tomlinson, 2008). Effective teachers engage in both formative and summative assessment to monitor and document student learning and inform their instruction. *Formative assessment* focuses on your use of inclusive classroom testing and assessment practices during instruction to monitor the learning progress of your students and to use this information to make ongoing decisions about the effectiveness of your teaching and ways you can improve it (Tomlinson, 2008). *Summative assessment* relates to your use of inclusive classroom tests and assessment products as a culminating activity at the end of instruction to assess student mastery of specific content, topics, concepts, and skills taught, and to communicate information about students' performance to others (Chappuis & Chappuis, 2008). Figure 0.2 presents a summary of the differences between formative and summative assessment.

Figure 0.2 A Summary of the Differences Between Formative and Summative Assessment

Formative Assessment	Summative Assessment
• Occurs on an ongoing basis during instruction • Assessment for student learning and to examine and improve instruction • Classroom-based and nongraded learning activities (quizzes, questions, observation, assignments) • Analyzed to provide information about student learning and instruction • Used to guide and adjust daily instruction and give feedback • Used more specifically by teachers and students	• Occurs at the end of instruction • Assessment to document student learning and to assess the effectiveness of instruction • High-stakes and teacher-made tests and graded culminating assignments aligned to learning standards • Statistical analysis to show student learning, students' grades, and program effectiveness • Used more globally by teachers and schools and to communicate with others

Source: Chappuis & Chappuis, 2008; Tomlinson, 2008.

Element: Inclusive classroom testing and assessment practices are integral parts of instructional planning (Childre, Sands, & Tanner Pope, 2009; Price & Nelson, 2007; Tomlinson, 2008; Yell, Busch, & Rogers, 2007). Your use of the best practices presented in this book should be an integral part of your instructional planning. Therefore, like Ms. Rodriguez, as you plan your units of instruction and individual lessons, you should first identify your instructional goals and use them to determine if you are going to evaluate your students' learning and your teaching using classroom tests or assessments or a combination of the two.

Element: Inclusive classroom testing and assessment practices involve collaboration between teachers, students, and families (Byrnes, 2008; Garcia & Ortiz, 2006; Salend, 2008). Like Ms. Rodriguez, your use of inclusive classroom testing and assessment practices will be enhanced by your collaboration with colleagues as well as your students and their families. Important information and decisions to guide your use of these practices can be obtained from a team. In addition to yourself and your students and their families, the team may include

- other teachers who work with your students;
- professionals who have knowledge of the learning standards, educational assessment, curriculum, and instruction; and
- culturally sensitive professionals and community members who understand how cultural, experiential, and linguistic factors impact assessing and instructing students.

Element: Inclusive classroom testing and assessment practices are consistent with No Child Left Behind (NCLB) and the Individuals with Disabilities Education Improvement Act (IDEIA; Byrnes, 2008; Ketterlin-Geller, Alonzo, et al., 2007; Towles-Reeves, Kleinert, & Muhomba, 2009; Yell, Katsiyannas, & Shriner, 2006). Although this book does not focus on high-stakes testing, it is important that your use of inclusive classroom testing and assessment practices be consistent with the provisions of NCLB and IDEIA. NCLB mandates the use of tests that are linked to learning standards and benchmarks tied to grade level standards in the general education curriculum for *all* of your students. IDEIA, which guides the delivery of a free and appropriate education to students with disabilities, recognizes that many of your students with disabilities will need testing accommodations to take tests (see Chapter 2) and that some of your students with more significant cognitive disabilities will need you to use alternative assessment methods to assess their learning and progress (see Chapter 5).

IDEIA calls for the use of *individuals-first* language when referring to individuals with disabilities (i.e., using the term *students with learning disabilities* rather than *learning disabled students*). Although I have used individuals-first language in this book, I also have tried to respect the preferences of some groups regarding what they like to be called. For instance, the National Association of the Deaf's Web site states that,

> Overwhelmingly, deaf and hard of hearing people prefer to be called "deaf" or "hard of hearing." Nearly all organizations of the deaf use the term "deaf and hard of hearing," and the National Association of the Deaf (NAD) is no exception. The World Federation of the Deaf (WFD) voted in 1991 to use "deaf and hard of hearing" as an official designation. (http://www.nad.org/)

Element: Inclusive classroom testing and assessment practices should be continuously evaluated (Cox, Herner, Demczyk, & Nieberding, 2006; Ketterlin-Geller, Alonzo, et al., 2007). Your use of inclusive classroom testing and assessment practices should be continually evaluated to determine if they are effective. Therefore, it is important to examine their impact on your students and their families as well as on yourself and your colleagues. Primarily, their effectiveness should be examined based on their impact on student learning, such as increased mastery of learning standards, positive changes in student grades, and improved state, districtwide, and classroom test results.

You and your colleagues can reflect on the impact of these practices in supporting your students' learning and informing your instruction. Your students and their family members can also provide information to share their viewpoints and to identify successful and unsuccessful practices. Testing and assessment practices that are not achieving their intended outcomes should be revised to make them more effective.

Another important factor to consider when evaluating these practices is *acceptability,* the extent to which a practice is easy to use, reasonable, fair, and appropriate for you and your students (Salend, 2008). As you read and learn about the best practices presented in each chapter of this book, consider their acceptability by asking the following questions:

- Is the practice consistent with my philosophy and the philosophical beliefs of others?
- Is the practice easy to implement?
- Is the practice age-appropriate?
- Does the practice require me to make significant changes in my teaching?
- Do I have the materials, time, resources, and technology needed to implement the practice?
- Which other individuals—educators, administrators, family members—do I need to support implementation of the practice?
- What skills and education do I and my students need to implement the practice?
- How will the practice affect specific students? Classmates? My colleagues? Family members?

Element: Inclusive classroom testing and assessment practices are evolving. Since inclusive classroom testing and assessment practices are constantly being developed and refined, you need to continue to learn more about them, including new strategies, technologies, and research. You can do this by reading the references and viewing Web sites cited in this book. You can attend conferences and professional development sessions, take courses, join professional organizations, and participate in Listservs and other online information gathering and sharing activities.

SPECIAL FEATURES

This book has several features designed to foster your use of classroom testing and assessment practices with *all* of your students. These special features include the following:

Chapter Opening Vignettes and Reflective Questions: Classroom case studies or comments appearing at the beginning of each chapter that present you with an overview and examples of the best practices presented in the chapter. After you read them, you will see questions that prompt you to reflect on the issues presented and your practices.

Chapter Questions: Questions serving as advance organizers to introduce you to the content and structure of each chapter.

Keys to Best Practices: Text boxes highlighting the best practices presented in each chapter.

Examples of Best Practices: Classroom examples presenting applications of the best practices presented within each chapter.

Reflectlists: Checklists summarizing the best practices presented within each chapter and prompting you to reflect on your use of these best practices and to explore ways you can incorporate them into your teaching.

Coming Attractions: A section appearing at the end of each chapter that introduces you to the content of the upcoming chapters.

1

Creating and Grading Valid and Accessible Teacher-Made Tests

Ms. Dodd was surprised and disappointed by her students' performance on her tests. While their performance during classroom learning activities indicated that her students understood the concepts and skills she was teaching, many of her students' test scores showed quite the opposite. A confused and frustrated Ms. Dodd asked her students to write, without signing their names, why they got the grades they did on her test. Students wrote the following:

"Your tests don't cover the material we learned in class."

"We spent all this time learning about one topic and there was only one question on that topic."

"I can't remember all the things you want us to know on one test."

"I accidentally skipped over some questions I could answer because there were too many questions on a page."

"I didn't have enough room to write my answers."

"I didn't understand what I was asked to do on some of the questions."

"A lot of the questions were tricky and confused me."

Ms. Dodd used her students' comments to improve her tests. She determined that it would be better if she tested her students more frequently on smaller amounts of information rather than giving them fewer tests covering a lot of information. She identified the content of her tests by listing the most important topics and concepts she taught as well as the percentage of instructional time she devoted to teaching them. She also asked her students to compose possible test questions and put some of their questions on future tests.

Ms. Dodd decided to use a balance of objective and essay test questions. As she wrote her questions, she made sure the language and sentence structures used were appropriate for her students and that they did not contain clues that helped students guess the correct answer. She highlighted key words in items and paired some of the text with visual images she downloaded from the Internet. To guide her students in responding to the essay questions, she listed the important vocabulary and concepts she wanted them to discuss.

To help her students pay attention to and understand directions, she presented the directions in text boxes bordered by white space. At different places throughout the test, she put reminders to prompt and encourage her students to ask questions if they didn't understand something. She carefully organized her test items in a consistent and uncluttered way to help her students avoid

(Continued)

(Continued)

skipping lines and test items. She made sure that her students had enough space to answer test items without having to continue writing on another page.

As students worked on the test, she observed them and noticed that they seemed to be more focused and less anxious. After she graded the test, she performed an item analysis to identify which test items were too difficult or too simple, tricky, or confusing. She was pleased that most of her test items were good ones and that her students' test performance matched her expectations for them.

- How do you and your students feel about your tests?
- What factors do you consider in designing your tests?
- How could you improve your tests?

High-quality teacher-made tests can aid you and your students in several ways. They can help you communicate to your students and their families important aspects of your curriculum and motivate your students to learn the concepts and skills you have taught. Your tests also can inform your teaching by identifying curricular areas mastered by your students as well as those that require additional or modified instruction. Test performance can be used to provide feedback to your students about their learning.

As the comments of Ms. Dodd's students reflect, the degree to which these benefits are likely to occur for you and your students depends on the quality of the tests you create. Teacher-made tests may be especially a challenge for those students who may struggle with the content and format of tests because of their attention, memory, organizational, language, reading, and writing difficulties, including your students with disabilities and second language learners (Salend, 2008). Therefore, this chapter offers a variety of best practices you can use to create and grade valid and accessible teacher-made tests that enhance the testing experience for all of your students (examples of these practices are presented in the text and in Figures 1.2–1.6 on pp. 25–33). Once you create good test questions using the information presented in this chapter, you can save them for use in the future.

Specifically, this chapter addresses the following questions:

- What factors should I consider in determining the content of my tests?
- How can I foster the readability and legibility of my tests?
- How can I format my tests to help my students to be organized and motivated and to pay attention?
- How can I help my students understand and follow test directions?
- How can I compose understandable, useful, valid, and appropriate test items?
- How can I grade my teacher-made tests?

WHAT FACTORS SHOULD I CONSIDER IN DETERMINING THE CONTENT OF MY TESTS?

One of the most important decisions you will make when creating your tests is determining the content that the test will assess. In choosing content for your tests, you want to be sure that your tests have *validity*. Tests that are not valid measures of your curriculum will be of little value to you in assessing your students' learning and enhancing your teaching.

Keys to Best Practice: Ensure that the content of your tests reflects your curriculum and assesses the most important topics, concepts, and skills you have taught (Hogan, 2007).

Validity

Validity refers to the extent to which the test measures what you want it to assess. In particular, it is important for you to make sure that your tests have *content validity*, which relates to the extent to which your test items cover and reflect your curriculum and the most important topics, concepts, and skills you taught and now want to assess. You can evaluate the content validity of your tests by examining the relationship between your test items and the topics and goals within your curriculum by asking the following questions:

- What content does my test assess?
- Is the content of the test complete and reflective of the curriculum and the important skills and concepts I have taught?
- Do test items allow students to demonstrate their knowledge and mastery of important topics and essential skills?
- Do the test items reflect my instructional objectives and priorities?
- Are there a sufficient number of items addressing my instructional objectives and priorities?
- Are test items sequenced from easiest to hardest?

You also can link test content directly to your curriculum by using curriculum-based measurement and the other assessment alternatives we will discuss in Chapter 5.

Keys to Best Practice: Test content should be consistent with the instructional strategies you used to help your students learn (Popham, 2006).

The content of your tests should be consistent with the instruction strategies you used to help your students learn. As such, your test items should reflect not only what but also how content has been taught. For example, content taught via role plays, simulations, cooperative learning, and problem-solving techniques is best tested through essay questions, whereas factual learning taught through teacher-directed activities may best be tested by objective test items such as multiple-choice questions. Additionally, the language you use to present both test directions and items should be consistent with that used in class.

Keys to Best Practice: Weight important topics more heavily so that the content assessed by your tests reflects the level of difficulty of the content as well as the amount of instructional time your class spent learning specific material (Salend, 2008).

You can enhance the validity of your tests by weighting the content of your tests to reflect the complexity of the concepts you taught and the amount of instructional time you devoted to teaching them. In other words, the percentage and number of items on a test assessing mastery of specific topics should be directly related to the levels of difficulty as well as the amount of class time you spent teaching that material. For instance, if you spent several days teaching about photosynthesis, then a corresponding percentage of your test questions should address students' mastery of content related to photosynthesis. Like Ms. Dodd, you can start to identify the content for your test by listing the topics and concepts you want the test to cover and then determining their levels of difficulty and importance as well as the percentage of instructional time you devoted to teaching them.

Keys to Best Practice: Focus the content of your tests by using more frequent tests that assess specific content rather than fewer tests covering a broader scope (Salend, 2008).

As Ms. Dodd realized, frequent tests that assess specific content, rather than fewer tests covering a broader scope, can foster validity and be beneficial for you and your students. It allows you to create tests that more thoroughly assess the specific content you have taught. More frequent tests have the advantage of offering students opportunities to develop effective test-taking skills and also help students who have difficulty remembering large amounts of information.

Keys to Best Practice: Involve students in determining the content of tests by asking them to identify important topics and compose possible test questions (Levine, 2003).

Like Ms. Dodd's students, your students can be a good source for identifying content for your tests. You can have your students work in groups to identify important topics that have been covered. You also can assign homework that asks students to compose possible test questions. This serves the dual purpose of helping your students to study and review their notes and textbook readings and providing you with a bank of potential questions. You can survey students at the beginning of a unit to determine what questions they have about important topics. To assist students in writing test items, you can review with them the content of the test as well as the qualities of good test questions (which we will discuss later in this chapter).

HOW CAN I FOSTER THE READABILITY AND LEGIBILITY OF MY TESTS?

Keys to Best Practice: Use a variety of strategies and technologies to enhance the readability and legibility of your testing materials (Salend, 2009; Sperling, 2006).

Testing materials that are difficult for students to read can cause problems for them, especially those of your students with reading, language, and learning difficulties (Sperling, 2006). Students who have difficulty reading your tests will have problems comprehending the test's directions and items. As a result, they may not be able to answer questions correctly, even when they have mastered the material you are testing. You can increase the accessibility of your tests for your students by enhancing the readability and legibility of your testing materials and formatting them appropriately so that they help your students stay organized and focused. Using technology can help you achieve these goals.

Keys to Best Practice: Foster the readability of your tests by carefully paying attention to your language and the types and number of words and sentence structures you use (Kozen, Murray, & Windell, 2006; Thompson, Johnstone, & Thurlow, 2002).

Fostering Readability

Readability refers to the linguistic factors that affect the ease with which students can read your text-based materials. The readability of your test items and directions can be fostered by carefully paying attention to your language as well as to the types and numbers of words and sentence structures you use. Therefore, as Ms. Dodd did, you can increase the readability of your testing materials by

- being as brief and direct as possible;
- using easy-to-understand language;
- offering examples that explain statements;
- eliminating unnecessary words and limiting the use of different words and prepositional phrases;
- referring directly to important points, objects, or events rather than using pronouns;
- presenting text in a tense and voice your students can comprehend;
- using sentence structures that are clear, explicit, and recognizable to students;
- having each sentence focus on only one main point;
- highlighting key words, terms, and concepts within sentences;
- embedding definitions or examples of important or difficult terminology into sentences;
- minimizing the length of sentences and paragraphs by deleting unnecessary clauses and phrases and by dividing long sentences into two or more sentences;
- avoiding the use of double negatives, abbreviations, contractions, acronyms, quotations, and parentheses;
- beginning paragraphs with a topic sentence; and
- having clear transitions and connections between sentences and paragraphs.

Keys to Best Practice: Use software programs to make sure that the readability of your tests is appropriate for your students (Salend, 2009).

Using Readability Software Programs

After you initially develop your tests, you can check to make sure that their readability is appropriate for your students by using software programs that determine the readability of text (see Figure 1.1). Many of these resources can help you revise your tests to make them more readable for your students. For example, readability programs can identify difficult words that can then be replaced with synonyms that are more appropriate for your students. In addition, most word processing programs provide access to readability formulas as well as strategies for enhancing a selection's readability. For instance, the automatic summarizing feature in many word processing programs (e.g., AutoSummarize in Microsoft Word) can help you condense and summarize test sections into shorter versions. Since readability software programs only assess readability in terms of the number of syllables (or letters) in a word and the number of words in a sentence, it is important to use them critically and as a guide. When using them, you should remember that the content-based terms that are being assessed by your tests cannot and should not be simplified.

Figure 1.1 Test Creation Resource Web Sites

Readability Formula Resources

Micro Power and Light Company (www.micropowerandlight.com)

ReadabilityStudio (www.oleandersolutions.com/readabilitystudio.html)

Online Readability Software (www.readability.online-web-software.com/demo.php)

Fryinator Readability Software (www.geocities.com/fryinator)

Readability Formulas (www.readabilityformulas.com)

Integrating Visual Supports Into Tests Resources

BoardMaker and Writing with Symbols (www.mayer-johnson.com)

Intellipics (www.synapseadaptive.com/intellitools)

Image Sharing Resources

Library of Congress Photographs Online Catalog (www.loc.gov/rr/print/catalog.html)

Flickr (www.flickr.com)

Picsearch (www.picsearch.com)

Item Analysis Resources

Assessment Systems (www.assess.com/xcart/home.php?cat=19)

Logic Extension Resources (www.lxr.com/site/home.aspx)

Open Office (www.openoffice.org)

Excel (www.office.microsoft.com/en-us/excel/default.aspx)

Gnumeric (http://projects.gnome.org/gnumeric)

Keys to Best Practice: Pair test text with visual supports such as pictures, graphics, and symbols (Abell, Bauder, & Simmons, 2004; Beddow, Kettler, & Elliott, 2008).

Pairing Visual Supports With Text

Pairing test text with visual supports such as pictures, graphics, and symbols can enhance the reading process and make your testing materials more readable, understandable, and motivating. In turn, this can promote your students' on-task behavior during testing situations. Embedding visuals in tests can enhance the test performance of students who have difficulty reading, hearing, or understanding

English. For instance, the accessibility of science tests can be fostered by providing students with graphics of a phenomena or an experiment followed by a series of related test questions (Abell et al., 2004).

However, always keep in mind that some students may be distracted by too many visuals and unnecessary stimuli. Therefore, when determining which and how many visual supports to use, you should make sure they are necessary and well-placed by considering whether they

- promote the readability and legibility of the test;
- explain, highlight, supplement, or summarize the testing materials;
- are linked to the text;
- are integrated appropriately within the test item;
- convey the intended information;
- assist students in identifying and comprehending important information;
- are self-explanatory or labeled appropriately;
- enhance the quality and visual presentation of the test without distracting students;
- prompt students to engage in and maintain on-task behavior; and
- are current, age-appropriate, and culturally sensitive (Beddow et al., 2008).

You can use a range of software and hardware to integrate visual supports into your tests (Parette, Wojcik, Peterson-Karlan, & Hourcade, 2005). Software programs provide access to a collection of graphics, photos, and picture communication symbols that can be paired with text (see Figure 1.1). You can also use digital cameras and computer graphics to integrate visual images into your tests to help students understand and pay attention to the test's directions and items. Like Ms. Dodd, you can use the image searching features available in most search engines or specialized image-sharing resources (see Figure 1.1) to identify appropriate and relevant pictures and images for use in your tests.

Fostering Legibility

Another critical factor that will affect your students' ability to read your tests is *legibility*. Whereas readability focuses on the linguistic variables that affect the ease of reading, *legibility* relates to the layout, format, organization, size, and appearance of the text, pictorials, and graphics in your tests. Technology can help you improve the legibility of your tests by offering resources for applying the principles of typographic and visual design, and formatting tests to foster your students' organizational, attention, and test-taking skills.

Keys to Best Practice: Apply the principles of typographic and visual design to create testing materials that are legible, organized, and formatted appropriately (Acrey, Johnstone, & Milligan, 2005; Salend, 2009).

Applying the Principles of Typographic and Visual Design

The principles of typographic and visual design can help you create testing materials that are legible, organized, and formatted appropriately. These principles, which are presented below and available via use of most word processing programs, can enhance the testing experience for students by facilitating understanding and speed.

Type Size: Type that is too small makes it difficult for your students to read, and type that is too large may cause their eyes to make excessive movements so that they pause more frequently. Therefore, it is suggested that your tests be composed using 12- to 14-point type. However, it is recommended that test text for students who are starting to read or who have visual difficulties be at least 18-point type.

Typefaces and Fonts: The legibility of your tests can be enhanced by your selection of typefaces and fonts that are familiar to your students and avoiding a mix of typefaces and fonts. Sans serif fonts such as Arial are good choices for students with reading difficulties because they look more like hand lettering, which can facilitate letter and word identification.

Case: Test text should be printed in lowercase and capital letters when grammatically appropriate because lowercase letters are easier for your students to discriminate and ALL CAPITAL TEXT OFTEN CAUSES STUDENTS TO READ MORE SLOWLY.

Style: Uninterrupted text presented in stylistic features such as *italics* and **boldface** slows the reading process. Therefore, stylistic variants should be used cautiously, sparingly, and only to **emphasize** and *highlight* small amounts of text embedded in sentences (e.g., highlighting key words in test directions or items) or to make brief headings more noticeable (e.g., highlighting headings that introduce directions for sections of the test). In general, it is more desirable to use color, italics, and boldface rather than underlining to highlight important text, as underlining can distract your students and make it harder for them to discriminate letters (e.g., *y* as *v* or *u* and *g* as *a*).

Line Length: Since line lengths can affect students' reading fluency, it is recommended that you present test text in line lengths of approximately four inches. You can do this by presenting text so that each line contains between 40 and 70 characters, or 7 to 12 words. When it is critical to present a series of text together in order to provide the context for understanding it (e.g., sentence completion and true-false items), try to present word clusters on the same line.

Spacing and Sequencing: Inappropriate spacing and sequencing of text can cause your students to become confused, disorganized, and frustrated. Therefore, you should try to examine the impact of all spaces on a test and make adjustments to make sure that the overall spacing is consistent and provides a logical structure for students and helps them make transitions from item to item. Providing students with enough space for written responses can help structure the length of their answers and facilitate their performance by not requiring them to continue writing on another page.

Justification: A test's legibility can be fostered by using left-aligned text and ragged right margins. It is suggested that you avoid justified text as it causes uneven word and letter spacing of text, which can cause your students to experience problems tracking the flow of text. Since centered text slows the reading process, it should be used selectively such as for titles or lists. Using a wider margin at the bottom of the page and numbering the pages can support student performance by helping them stay organized.

Background and Contrast: Your tests' backgrounds and contrast can impact your students' success in reading and completing them. Therefore, the color of the text and background should be markedly different so that it will be easier for students to identify and focus on critical information. You can enhance the background and contrast of your tests by printing it using black or blue text on an off-white, pale, or matte pastel background.

You can focus your students' attention on important aspects of tests by surrounding those aspects with white space or by embedding them in thick and dark borders. For example, important directions or test items can be placed in text boxes that are bordered by white space.

HOW CAN I FORMAT MY TESTS TO HELP MY STUDENTS TO BE ORGANIZED AND MOTIVATED AND TO PAY ATTENTION?

Keys to Best Practice: Format tests to help your students stay organized and pay attention (Acrey et al., 2005; Beddow et al., 2008; Salend, 2008).

Formatting Tests to Support Organization and Attention

Test materials that are poorly formatted and disorganized can hinder readability and legibility and overwhelm your students and affect their attention and motivation. For instance, one of Ms. Dodd's students said that having too many items on a page resulted in accidentally skipping over questions. This is especially true for your students who have organizational and attention difficulties. The following are ways you can format your tests to help your students stay organized and pay attention:

- Limit the number of items on a page and limit clutter by providing sufficient blank space between items.
- Present items in a natural, fixed, organized, symmetrical, and simple numbered sequence to guide students in making transitions from one item to another. Having a clearly predictable and delineated sequence throughout the test can help your students avoid skipping lines and test items.
- Group similar question types together.
- Sequence items from easiest to hardest to help motivate students and keep them from becoming frustrated.
- Place test items and the directions for completing them on the same page so that students do not have to be distracted by turning back and forth.
- Reduce the confusion that can occur when students are asked to transfer items to a separate answer sheet by having students write their answers on the test itself.
- Provide students with sufficient space to answer test items without having to continue writing on another page. An appropriate amount of space between items can serve to structure the length of their responses.
- Give students some space between questions so that they can write a rationale or clarification for their responses to these items.
- Offer students scrap paper or space to perform a memory dump or download of important information and mnemonics they studied (we will learn more about effective study and test-taking behaviors in Chapter 4).
- Present sequenced information in chronological order through use of numbers or the words *first, second,* and *third.*
- Employ bullets to present essential information that does not have a numerical or hierarchical order.

Keys to Best Practice: Format tests to provide students with strategy, encouragement, and motivation prompts and reminders (Salend, 2009).

Providing Strategy, Encouragement, and Motivation Prompts and Reminders

Your students may need strategy, encouragement, and motivation prompts and reminders to help them organize, remember, and retrieve important content, solve problems, and complete tasks independently (Lenz, 2006). Therefore, when appropriate, you can format your tests to prompt and remind students to use such test-taking strategies as reviewing and asking questions about test items and directions, paying attention to emphasized or highlighted information, understanding context cues, and constructing mental pictures. For instance, at the beginning of the essay question section of tests, you can provide students with a reminder to use ANSWER, a test-taking strategy designed to guide students in writing essay responses (Hughes, Schumaker, & Deshler, 2005). (See Figure 1.6 on p. 33.) Specific information about ANSWER and other test-taking strategies is presented in Chapter 4.

You also can embed motivating and encouraging words and icons throughout the test. These prompts and reminders can be especially helpful for students who experience anxiety when taking tests. (We will learn more about how you can try to minimize test anxiety in Chapter 4.) At the beginning of the test, you can include a statement and graphics that encourage students to do well and to work hard to show all they have learned in class. As Ms. Dodd did throughout her test, you can periodically place prompts to remind students to stay focused and motivated and to engage in self-reinforcement (e.g., *Are you doing your best? Tell yourself you are doing well and give yourself a pat on the back*), to seek clarification (e.g., *Do you have any questions about the test?*), to follow directions (e.g., *Remember to write in complete sentences*), and to alert them to the length of the test and to relax (e.g., *Smile. You are halfway through the test*). At the end of the test, you can congratulate them (e.g., *Way to go. Congratulations on finishing the test*), and remind them to review each question and their answers (e.g., *Did you check all of your answers?*). Additional suggestions for using technology-based testing to motivate your students when taking your tests are provided in Chapter 3.

HOW CAN I HELP MY STUDENTS UNDERSTAND AND FOLLOW TEST DIRECTIONS?

In addition to the guidelines we just discussed, you can help your students understand and follow directions by using the guidelines presented below to introduce important aspects of your test and carefully phrase and present directions for test items. We will discuss specific guidelines for presenting directions for specific types of questions later in this chapter.

Keys to Best Practice: Clearly introduce important aspects of tests (McLoughlin & Lewis, 2008; Overton, 2009).

Introducing the Test

You can increase the accessibility of your tests and help your students perform better on your tests if you give them an overview of the important parts of tests, such as the overall directions and rules. When introducing a test, convey a positive attitude toward the test and make certain that *all students* are attentive, pausing when they are not. Try to keep your introduction as brief as possible (remember some students will be nervous and anxious to start taking the test), and orally highlight key words and statements.

Begin by describing the test and the reasons for taking it. Next, share important aspects about the test by reviewing the overall directions. To ensure that students understand the test's directions, you can, at the beginning of the test, assign several practice items relating to the various types of questions on the test. These practice items can be reviewed with students before allowing them to proceed with the rest of the test. If new types of questions or answer sheets are being used on the test, clearly identify and explain them, highlighting their novel aspects. You also can explain the breakdown of points for specific items and sections and remind students to work on those sections worth the most points in descending order.

Your introduction should alert students to the rules that will be in effect during testing and remind them of the importance of academic honesty. Rules should specify the testing behaviors allowed by students, the materials they are allowed to use, and the procedures they should follow to ask questions, seek assistance, and go to the bathroom. Prior to beginning the testing, you should make sure that students' physical needs (medications, hunger, thirst, or use of the bathroom) have been addressed. You can remind students to use good test-taking skills, and you can ensure that testing accommodations have been implemented and that specialized devices and technology that students use are working properly.

It helps to encourage your students to ask questions about the overall test and to ask them to paraphrase and explain important or novel directions, procedures, and rules. You may want to assess their comprehension of the following:

- *Directions and rules* ("What directions and rules are you expected to follow when working on this test?" "Can you think of any problems you might have in completing this test?" "What should you do if you have a problem?")
- *Materials they need and can use to complete the test* ("What materials do you need?" "What materials can you use?")
- *Ways they can obtain clarification or assistance* ("If you have a question or experience a problem, what should you do?")
- *Point totals for specific questions and sections* ("Which sections are worth the most points? How many points is the essay question worth?")
- *Time limit for completing the test* ("How long do you have to work on the test?")
- *Things they can do if they finish early* ("What can you do if you finish early?")
- *Questions they may have about the test* ("Do you have any questions about the test before we begin?")

If you have students who typically experience some difficulties following directions, you can have them complete several items under your supervision before beginning to work independently. You also can periodically monitor their performance and structure the testing so that these students work on one specific section at a time and check with you before going on to the next section.

Keys to Best Practice: Clearly and carefully phrase and present directions for test items (Conderman & Koroghlanian, 2002; Salend, 2008).

Phrasing and Presenting Directions for Test Items

As Ms. Dodd's students' comments indicated, it is extremely important for teachers to clearly phrase and present directions for each section of the test that contains different types of items (see Figures 1.2–1.6 on pp. 25–33 for examples of best practices for phrasing and presenting directions). When phrasing and presenting directions and items, consider the following:

- Use easy-to-understand language that is familiar to students (e.g., instead of asking students to compare and contrast two concepts, you can ask them to write how the concepts are alike and different).
- Avoid vague terms that may confuse students or be subject to multiple interpretations (e.g., *frequently*, *usually*) and eliminate unnecessary information.
- Include statements that specify the precision you expect students to provide when answering. For example, directions for a section on measuring angles should include a statement defining that, in order to be correct, students' measurements must be within a specific number of degrees.
- List the point totals associated with items and sections prominently. Providing this information can help students develop a plan and timeline for completing tests based on the point values associated with specific items and sections of tests.
- Check test directions and items to make sure that they do not contain clues that can unintentionally lead to guessing the correct response. Proofread your tests to make sure that they do not include

  grammatical cues (e.g., the articles *a* and *an*, plurals);

  word cues (e.g., the same words appear in the question and answer); and

  similarity cues (e.g., the information in one question leads to the answers in other questions).

When presenting directions that have several steps, it is helpful to number and list the steps in sequential order (see Figures 1.3–1.5 on pp. 25–31). For example, a test item related to latitude and longitude can be presented by listing the following steps:

1. Identify the city on the map.

2. Use the map to determine the city's latitude and longitude.

3. Use the appropriate format to write the coordinates for the city's latitude and longitude.

Keys to Best Practice: Use technology to help your students focus on and pay attention to test directions (Salend, 2009).

Using Technology

You can use technology to help your students focus on and pay attention to test directions. Via technology you can use cues (circling, color coding, font variations, underlining, italicizing, boldfacing, enlarging) and graphics to *highlight* critical aspects of directions by

- presenting important directions and a correct model of each type of test item in text boxes that are bordered by white space as Ms. Dodd did in the chapter opening vignette (see Figures 1.2–1.5 on pp. 25–33);
- displaying direction reminders at important locations throughout the test (e.g., *Remember to write clearly and to use complete sentences*; see Figures 1.5 and 1.6 on pp. 31 and 33);
- using color-coded arrows to alert students to pay attention to the directions for a new set of test items; and
- embedding symbols, icons, pictorials, reminders, or signs at various sections of the test to direct and prompt students. For example, *go* signs can be used to encourage students to continue to keep working, and *stop* signs can indicate the end of a section.

As we discussed previously, you can use software and digital cameras to present computer-based activity directions, which employ combinations of pictures, graphics, symbols, and words to aid your students in comprehending and following sequential directions (Stromer, Kimball, Kinney, & Taylor, 2006).

HOW CAN I COMPOSE UNDERSTANDABLE, USEFUL, VALID, AND APPROPRIATE TEST ITEMS?

Test items are the most critical part of any test. Unfortunately, writing understandable, useful, appropriate, and valid test questions is very difficult. As mentioned earlier, it is essential that you make sure that test items assess the most important and relevant concepts and skills you have taught. In addition, your test items should be consistent with the instructional strategies you used to help your students learn.

Keys to Best Practice: Consider if it is appropriate to match the content and format of your test questions with the high-stakes tests your students will take (Hogan, 2007).

Although it is not appropriate to "teach to the test," you can consider whether it is appropriate to match the content and format of test questions on your teacher-made tests with the high-stakes tests your students will take. That way, you can assess student performance while at the same time helping students become more familiar with the conditions they will encounter when taking high-stakes tests.

Keys to Best Practice: Make your test questions motivating, creative, challenging, and relevant to your students' lives and academic abilities (Savage, Savage, & Armstrong, 2006).

It helps to use test questions that are motivating, challenging, and relevant to your students' lives and academic abilities. When possible, you can motivate your students and personalize your tests by phrasing items using the students' and teachers' names (make sure that individuals will not be embarrassed or object to having their names used in questions). You also can personalize your tests by incorporating students' interests and experiences as well as integrating popular characters, items, and trends in test items. Science, English, and social studies questions can be related to local sites and museums, and math word problems can be presented using names and persons, places, and things associated with their community. For example, the essay question in Figure 1.6 on page 33 asks students to apply and share their knowledge of food groups and healthy foods choices by responding from the perspective of being on a schoolwide committee examining healthy school meals. You can motivate and challenge your students by presenting them with creative test items that incorporate suspense, fantasy, curiosity, uncertainty, and novelty.

Keys to Best Practice: Make sure your test questions are respectful and reflective of your students' individual differences (Beddow et al., 2008).

Inclusive tests contain test questions that are respectful and reflective of your students' individual differences related to race, linguistic ability, economic status, gender, ethnicity, cultural and religious backgrounds, family structure, and sexual orientation. Therefore, you need to make sure that your test questions assess content from a multicultural perspective and portray individuals and groups in realistic, factually correct, and nonstereotypic ways. You can make your test questions more inclusive and meaningful for your students by using a variety of culturally relevant referents and presenting and describing individuals and groups using appropriate terms.

When writing your test questions, you need to address the strengths and challenges of your students. Student performance on your tests can be improved by composing well-written, grammatically correct, challenging, and academically appropriate test items that students can read and understand. You can make your tests fairer for students by avoiding *hinging*, which refers to the use of items whose correct answers require students to answer preceding questions correctly (National Board of Medical Examiners, 2002).

Objective Test Items

Tests are usually made up of objective and essay test questions (which we will discuss later). Objective test questions, including multiple choice, matching, true-false, and sentence completion items, ask students to select or write a number, letter, word, or short phrase or sentence. Although objective items are typically used to assess students' memory and understanding of information, they also can be used to test simple problem solving and data interpretation as well as the application of rules (Brookhart & Nitko, 2008).

In addition to considering the recommendations for phrasing and presenting test directions we discussed previously, here are some guidelines that can help you compose your objective and essay test items. Sample items incorporating these guidelines are presented in Figures 1.2–1.6.

Keys to Best Practice: Use effective guidelines for composing multiple-choice items (Brookhart & Nitko, 2008; Hogan, 2007; National Board of Medical Examiners, 2002).

Composing Multiple-Choice Items

Multiple-choice items, which can be used to assess your students' application of content or recall of information, are the most common type of test items on teacher-made tests. These items are made up of the *stem,* which presents a question, statement, paragraph, or visual (e.g., chart, map) and the conditions associated with it, followed by a series of answer choices consisting of the correct answer as well as incorrect choices or *distractors.* When writing multiple-choice questions, you should pay careful attention to each item stem and the answer choices. The stem should

- present the conditions associated with the item and provide a context for answering it;
- address only one major point related to important content from the curriculum;
- focus only on the information students need to answer the question and avoid unnecessary information;
- be free of idiomatic expressions, jargon, and extraneous verbiage;
- be written so that students can answer it without looking at the answer choices;
- be longer than the answer choices so that you don't have to repeat content from the stem when presenting your answer choices;
- be written in the active voice; and
- be stated in the positive. In the limited number of cases in which you use a negative stem, it is suggested that you highlight the negative words (e.g., *not, except*) and briefly phrase your answer choices as single words, short phrases, or sentences.

The answer choices should have the following characteristics:

- They should have only one correct answer.
- They should contain three to five letter- or number-based response alternatives. Increasing the number of response choices reduces the likelihood that students will be able to select the correct answer by guessing.
- They should not contain key words or phrases from the stem.
- They should be presented using a vertical format (unless students are used to working with a horizontal format) that presents each answer alternative on a separate indented line followed by a blank.
- They should be presented in a logical and thoughtful sequence such as by alphabetical, numerical, or chronological order. Since the correct numerical choice often is the middle number, it is best to include numeral choices that are closer to the middle number and the correct response and not at the extremes. Numerical data also should be presented in the same format. For example, all item choices should be presented in the format that is most appropriate for the item (e.g., whole numbers, percentages, ranges, decimals, fractions). When there is not an obvious sequence, randomly vary the correct answer in the answer alternative sequence and

make sure that you avoid predictable patterns (e.g., the correct answer is always C).

- They should be feasible, grammatically correct, and similar in length, completeness, and specificity. These factors are important to lessen the likelihood that students will select the correct answer based on a process of elimination or guessing by focusing on the choices' plausibility, grammar, wording, length, completeness, or detail. You also should avoid using meaningless and humorous answer alternatives.
- They should share common elements. For example, if the correct choice is a specific planet, then all of the choices should be planets. However, be careful to make sure that you do not tip off your students by phrasing the correct answer in a way that it shares more similar elements than the other choices. This is especially important when your answer choices contain two or more alternatives. For instance, if the response choices are (a) Saturn and Jupiter; (b) Saturn and Mars; (c) Jupiter and Uranus; and (d) Saturn and Neptune, the correct answer is most likely (a) Saturn and Jupiter because both Saturn and Jupiter appear in the other choices.
- They should be based on common error patterns and misunderstandings associated with the topic or skill. You can ask students to respond to open-ended versions of the multiple-choice questions and then use their most frequent errors and misunderstandings as distractors.
- They should not include categorical words and absolutes such as *always, all, only,* or *never.*

To avoid confusion, the stem and the answer choices should contain familiar, easy-to-understand language and direct sentences. These items should not assess students' opinions or values and should be free of double negatives. When using multiple-choice items to test vocabulary words and content specific terminology, the stem should contain the word, and the possible definitions should be listed in the answer choices (Brookhart & Nitko, 2008).

You can tailor your multiple-choice items for your students, particularly those with special needs, by

- highlighting keywords;
- decreasing the number of answer alternatives;
- eliminating confusing language;
- limiting the use of certain response alternatives such as having to select *all of the above* or *none of the above,* as using these types of response choices serves to make the question a series of true-false items (however, if you choose to use these types of choices, make sure they periodically serve as the correct response); and
- allowing students to circle the answer they choose rather than requiring them to transfer it to a separate answer sheet.

A sample multiple-choice item depicting many of these effective guidelines is presented in Figure 1.2.

Figure 1.2   Sample Multiple-Choice Item

Directions: Circle the letter of the choice that best answers the question. Each multiple-choice item is worth 3 points.

1. A poet writes, ***Bertha blew big, blue bubbles.*** What type of poetic device is the poet using?

   a. Alliteration

   b. Metaphor

   c. Onomatopoeia

   d. Personification

KEYS TO BEST PRACTICE

- Directions are clear and concise, include the visual cue of circling, and are presented in a text box.
- Students respond on the test by circling the letter of their choice.
- Students are informed of the point values associated with each item of this type.
- The item stem presents information related to only one major point and provides the context for answering the question.
- The item stem is stated in the positive without excess verbiage, longer than the answer choices, and important information in the item stem is highlighted.
- The correct choice is clearly the best answer.
- The answer choices share common elements, and are feasible, shorter than the item stem, of the same length, and presented alphabetically and vertically with appropriate lettering, indentation, and spacing.
- The answer choices do not include difficult choices such as *all of the above*, or *A and D*.
- There are no clues that can unintentionally lead students to guess or figure out the correct response.

Keys to Best Practice: Use effective guidelines for composing matching items (Brookhart & Nitko, 2008; Conderman & Koroghlanian, 2002; Hogan, 2007).

Composing Matching Items

Matching items are appropriate for testing students' mastery of relationships between two concepts or sets of information. Therefore, consider using matching items when you can create homogeneous lists of corresponding premises and responses that relate to a single theme or concept. When writing matching items, you should consider the following factors that can impact your students' performance (Hogan, 2007):

- Each matching section contains a maximum of 10 understandable, grammatically similar, and concise item pairs related to a single theme or topic.

If you feel it is necessary to assess more than 10 item pairs, the additional item pairs should be grouped by topic or content area and presented in separate matching sections.

- The matching section has two appropriately named columns made up of only one type of information or element and organized in a logical way (alphabetically, chronologically, numerical, etc.) with items listed in one column labeled with numbers and items presented in the other column labeled with letters.
- The matching section has one column that contains approximately 25% more items than the other column. When there are an equal number of items in each column, students may inadvertently get the last pair correct as it is the only pair left.
- The matching section contains feasible choices, and only one correct response for each pair is offered.
- The matching section is presented so that the longer items are listed in the left-hand column. Since most students work on matching items by reading an item in the left-hand column and then seeking the appropriate match by examining all the choices in the right-hand column, structuring your matching items in this way can help students maximize use of their time. For example, a matching item assessing key science terms should be presented so that the definitions are in the left-hand column and the terms are in the right-hand column.

Careful presentation of matching items is important for your students, especially those with special needs. Your directions for these items should help your students clearly understand the basis for matching the item pairs (Brookhart & Nitko, 2008). By placing the directions and both columns on the same page, you can prevent the possible confusion that can occur when students have to turn back and forth to match sections that appear on two different pages. You also can help students follow your directions by embedding an example of a correct response in the matching item. Your directions should inform students whether items from columns can be used more than once. Structuring these items so that students write the letter or number associated with their response choice on a blank line can avoid the confusion and disorganization that can occur when students are required to draw lines connecting the matched pairs from one column to another. A sample matching item depicting many of these effective guidelines is presented in Figure 1.3.

You can minimize the reading requirements associated with these items by presenting graphic or pictorial representations in one column. For example, in the sample matching item related to angles presented in Figure 1.3, you can present graphic representations of angles depicting the different types of angles such as

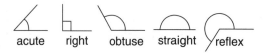

rather than their definitions in Column 1.

Figure 1.3 Sample Matching Item

Directions: Match each definition in Column 1 with its angle name in Column 2 using the following procedure:

1. Read the definition in Column 1.
2. Find its matching angle name in Column 2.
3. Write the letter of the angle name in Column 2 in the blank next to its definition in Column 1.

   - The first one is done for you as an example.
   - Remember that each type of angle may be selected once, more than once, or not at all.
   - Each correct match is worth 2 points.

Column 1: Angle Definitions

A__ 1. An angle that is less than 90 degrees

___ 2. An angle that is 90 degrees

___ 3. An angle that is greater than 90 and less than 180 degrees

___ 4. An angle that is 180 degrees

___ 5. An angle that is greater than 180 degrees and less than 360 degrees

Column 2: Angle Name

A. Acute angle

B. Corresponding angle

C. Obtuse angle

D. Reflex angle

E. Right angle

F. Straight angle

G. Supplementary angle

KEYS TO BEST PRACTICE

- Directions help students understand the basis for matching the item pairs and are presented in a text box with numbered steps to guide students.
- Directions inform students whether items from columns can be used more than once.
- Directions inform students of the point totals associated with item pairs.
- Directions and all aspects of the item are presented on the same page and include an example of a correct response.
- Students are provided with a blank in which to record the letter or number associated with their response choice rather than a drawing line.
- Columns contain fewer than 10 understandable, grammatically similar item pairs related to a single topic with longer item statements listed on the left, and shorter item statements on the right.
- Columns have been labeled appropriately and organized in a logical way with items listed in one column labeled with numbers and items presented in the other column labeled with letters.
- Columns contain feasible choices related to common elements with only one correct response for each pair and with approximately 25% more items in one column than in the other.

Keys to Best Practice: Use effective guidelines for composing true-false items (Brookhart & Nitko, 2008; Hogan, 2007; Salend, 2008).

Composing True-False Items

True-false items are used to test students' factual knowledge and understanding of whether aspects of concepts are presented correctly and completely.

Although these items typically are presented as statements that students identify as *true* or *false,* they also can be questions for which the response is *yes* or *no* (e.g., *Is it possible for a naturalized citizen to become president of the United States? Yes or No*).

Keep in mind that true-false items may not accurately reflect student mastery, since students have a 50% chance of guessing the correct answer. In addition, many students may encounter problems answering true-false items, especially when these items require them to make false statements true. You can try to minimize these problems and enhance the validity of your true-false items by using the following guidelines:

- Limit your use of true-false questions.
- Have each item address only one important point or relationship.
- Focus items on content related to material taught rather than intuition, common sense, or general knowledge.
- Phrase items as concise declarative statements that are clearly either true or false.
- Provide the relevant background information and context for answering the question.
- Present the source of the information (e.g., *According to our textbook*).
- Highlight important parts of items.
- Avoid the use of vague statements, terms, and phrases (e.g., *usually, probably, rarely, frequently, is useful for*), which can mean different things to different students; **qualifying words** (e.g., *often, may, can, sometimes, usually, frequently, generally*), which cue students that a statement is true; and **absolute words** (e.g., *always, all, every, entirely, only, never, none*), which indicate that a statement is false.
- State items positively and without double negatives. When items must be stated in the negative, highlight the **negative** words and phrases (e.g., *no, not, cannot*).
- Delete questions that assess mastery of nonessential content, skills, and facts (e.g., *George Washington chopped down a cherry tree. True or False*).
- Make sure items do not contain misleading and irrelevant information or ask students to make value judgments. When using items that require evaluative judgments, phrase items as evaluative statements (e.g., *Compared to . . . , it is . . .*).
- Write false statements based on common misconceptions associated with the topic being assessed.
- Make all true-false items of the same length, if possible.
- Group true-false items by content assessed.
- Link true-false items to interpretations of visuals such as graphs and maps and text-based materials.
- Write the response choices of *True or False* completely so that students can answer by circling either *True* or *False*, since some students may inadvertently confuse the *T* and the *F* when working in the pressure situation of a test.
- Watch for and avoid predictable answer patterns (e.g., TTFF or FTFT). You can do this by randomizing the sequence of true and false statements so that there are no obvious patterns and a similar number of statements that are true and false. Having an equal number of items that are true and false also can minimize the impact of guessing, as students tend to guess true more often than false.

A sample true-false item depicting many of these effective guidelines is in Figure 1.4.

Figure 1.4   Sample True-False Item

Directions:

1. Read each statement.
2. If the statement is **true**, circle True.
3. If the statement is **false**, circle False.
   - The first one is done for you as an example.
   - Each true-false item is worth 1 point.

Example: True or False   Cirrus clouds form at heights *greater* than *20,000 feet.*

    1. True or False A *meander* is a feature of a lake.

KEYS TO BEST PRACTICE

- Directions are clear and concise, include the visual cue of circling, and are presented in a text box with numbered steps to guide students.
- Students are provided with a correct model of the item type and informed of the point values associated with each item of this type.
- Response choices are written out, and students indicate their responses by circling either *True* or *False* rather than writing it out.
- Items measure one important concept, point, or relationship that was taught.
- Important information in the item statement is highlighted.
- Item statements are phrased concisely and positively and are free of vague terms, qualifying and absolute words, and double negatives.
- Items are unequivocally true or false.

Keys to Best Practice: Use effective guidelines for composing sentence completion items (Brookhart & Nitko, 2008; Hogan, 2007; Salend, 2008).

Composing Sentence Completion Items

Sentence completion items involve students writing or choosing a word or short phrase that best completes a sentence. Since sentence completion items frequently relate to information presented in print materials that can be vague when taken out of the context of a paragraph or chapter, you should make sure that the content being assessed is appropriate for this type of item. Rather than composing these items by copying the wording from textbooks and other instructional materials, paraphrase the information in language that is understandable to students. The following are some additional suggestions for writing sentence completion items that can help your students respond to these types of items.

- Make sure these items address important content and concepts and not trivial and vague information.
- Make sure that the omitted word or phrase is important and relevant.

- Use word blanks that require a one-word response. If word blanks must contain more than one word, limit the length to a short phrase.
- Locate word blanks near the end of the items.
- Have only one word blank per sentence.
- Keep word blanks the same length and use the same format. This helps you avoid giving students cues about the length of the word.
- Avoid giving grammatical cues. For example, use a(n) before a blank that is answered with a noun (e.g., *A narrow section of land that connects two larger portions of land is a(n)* isthmus).
- Determine if you will accept specific synonyms, abbreviations, and other possible variations as correct responses as well as misspellings. Be sure to let students know this in the written directions.
- Pair these items with a text box containing a word bank from which students can choose a response to complete the statement. Words in the word bank should share similar grammatical features (e.g., similar parts of speech, capitalization), be presented in a logical order (e.g., alphabetical, numerical order), and have proper spacing. Where possible, the words in word banks can be categorized and placed together in the list.
- Inform students if words from the word bank may be used more than once.

A sample sentence completion item depicting many of these effective guidelines is presented in Figure 1.5.

Keys to Best Practice: Use effective guidelines for composing essay questions (Brookhart & Nitko, 2008; Hogan, 2007; Salend, 2008).

Composing Essay Questions

In many teacher-made tests, objective questions tend to be predominant. However, essay test items are used to assess your students' in-depth mastery of content from your curriculum and their ability to apply these concepts. These items also allow your students to demonstrate their writing, higher-level thinking, creativity, and problem-solving skills, and to express their opinions. Like Ms. Dodd, you can improve the quality of your tests by having an appropriate balance between objective and essay test items.

Essay questions use either a restricted response format or an open-ended format (Brookhart & Nitko, 2008). Whereas restricted response essay items provide students with a structure that directs both the content and format of their essay (e.g., *What is the relationship between weathering and erosion? Provide examples to support your answer*), open-ended essay questions allow students greater leeway in the way they respond (e.g., *Imagine you are living in the South after Lee's surrender at Appomattox. Based on what we have learned, write a diary entry that describes the impact of Lee's surrender on you, your family, and your town*).

Because of the numerous skills students need to answer essay questions, you should try to create questions that are appropriate for a range of students, clearly state what you are asking students to do, and are understandable in terms of their readability and level of difficulty (use the readability and legibility guidelines discussed earlier in this chapter). When writing essay questions, you also should make sure they address important content from your curriculum and provide your students with the opportunity to apply their learning.

Figure 1.5 Sample Sentence Completion Item

Directions:

1. Read the sentence.
2. Look at the *word bank.*
3. Choose the word from the word bank that correctly completes the sentence.
   Each word in the word bank can be used only once.
4. Write the correct word on the blank at the end of sentence.
5. Write clearly so I can read it.
   Each correctly completed sentence is worth 1 point.

1. The subatomic particles inside an atom that have a ***positive*** charge are _____.
2. Isotopes are atoms of the ***same*** element that have ***different*** numbers of _____.

Word Bank

Compounds	Ions
Deuterons	Neutrons
Electrons	Protons

KEYS TO BEST PRACTICE

- Directions are clear and concise and are presented in a text box with numbered steps to guide students.
- Direction reminders are displayed in a prominent location (e.g. *Write clearly so I can read it*).
- Students are given a text box containing a word bank from which students can choose a response to complete the statement. Words in the word bank share similar grammatical features (e.g., similar parts of speech, capitalization), are presented in a logical order (e.g., alphabetical, numerical order), and have proper spacing.
- Students write their answers on the blank rather than transferring them to another page.
- Students are informed about whether they may use a word from the bank more than once, and about the point values associated with each item of this type.
- The word blanks require a one-word response, are located at the end of the sentence, are of the same length, and use the same format.
- Important content in the sentences is highlighted.
- Sentences and omitted words relate to relevant content and concepts that were taught.
- Items are presented using one sentence and one word blank and provide a sufficient context for answering the question correctly.
- Items are phrased so there is only one correct answer and grammatical cues are not provided.

Therefore, as Ms. Dodd did, you can plan and compose your essay questions based on your curricular goals and your students' abilities by using the following guidelines:

- Highlight key words that your students can use to analyze, structure, and write their answers.
- Specify the desired length of their response and your basis for evaluating it. When essay questions ask students to present their opinions, make sure that your students understand that they will be judged on their ability to support their opinion rather than the position they express.

- List important vocabulary and concepts to be addressed in the essays for students. Place these lists in prominent locations on your tests to make sure that your students will notice them before composing their responses.
- Break open-ended essay questions into smaller sequential subquestions. Using subquestions in lieu of a single open-ended essay question can help your students produce a more organized and complete answer.

A sample essay question depicting many of these effective guidelines is presented in Figure 1.6.

When memory of factual information is not an essential aspect of what you are testing, you can help your students understand and respond to essay items in several ways. You can define important concepts that students should include in their essays. When it is not possible to define a large number of words and concepts on the test itself, you can allow students to use a word list or dictionary. Additional testing accommodations that can help your students respond to essay questions are presented in Chapter 2.

HOW CAN I GRADE MY TEACHER-MADE TESTS?

Test grading provides you with a good opportunity to collect and analyze information about your students' learning and their test performance. This information also serves as an excellent way to inform your teaching and evaluate your tests. Below are guidelines to help you do this.

Keys to Best Practice: Create and use a complete scoring key or answer sheet (Brookhart & Nitko, 2008; Hogan, 2007; National Board of Medical Examiners, 2002).

Creating Scoring Keys or Answer Sheets

Begin grading your tests by creating a *scoring key*, also called an *answer sheet*, that lists the correct answers to specific questions and the points each question is worth. Since some of your test questions may have multiple correct answers, especially your essay questions, your scoring key can contain the range of responses you will consider correct as well as the guidelines you will use to award points for partially correct or incomplete answers. If you deduct points for incorrect answers, your scoring key should address these procedures.

Your scoring key is used to grade and score your students' tests and to obtain raw scores and percentages. Raw scores and percentages are important in helping you determine the mean, mode, median, and range of your students' scores on a test. The *mean* is the average of your students' scores on the test, the *mode* is the most frequently occurring score obtained by your students, and the *median* is the midpoint of your students' test scores. In looking at the class's performance, you can look at the difference between the lowest and highest scores, which is referred to as the *range*. By examining the mean, mode, median, and range, you can examine the distribution of your students' scores, which can help you see how your

Figure 1.6   Sample Essay Question

You have been asked to serve on the school's healthy foods committee. The committee is looking at ways to include healthy foods that students like on daily menus. At the first meeting, the group is going to discuss healthy foods from the different food groups. Prepare an essay of **between 300–400 words** that presents your suggestions for healthy foods from the different food groups. In writing your essay, consider the following:

- Identify and give examples of the foods that make up the different food groups.
- Explain why each food group is important and how many servings from each group one should have each day.
- Discuss what makes up healthful foods, what are some healthful foods from each food group that students might like, and why these healthful foods are good alternatives for students.
- Plan a healthy lunch menu for one day for our cafeteria.

- Use and discuss such terms as *calories, vitamins, sugars, proteins, minerals, grains, whole grains,* carbohydrates, antibiotics, hormone-free, fats, and trans-fats.
- Provide evidence and examples to support your statements and positions.
- Use correct grammar, punctuation, spelling, and paragraph organization.
- Use the **ANSWER** strategy to prepare your essay.
- Your essay is worth 25 points.

KEYS TO BEST PRACTICE

- Directions clearly explain and provide the context for answering the question and what students need to do, and specify the length of the essay.
- The question focuses on important content from the curriculum and asks students to apply their learning to an authentic situation that is relevant to students' lives.
- Subquestions that divide the essay question into smaller sequential items are provided to help students interpret the question correctly and to guide students in developing and writing their essays.
- Reminders and prompts are presented to students using a text box and graphics. Reminders and prompts relate to (a) the important vocabulary and concepts that students should use in writing their essays; (b) the importance of supporting their statements and positions and the importance of using correct grammar, punctuation, spelling, and paragraph organization; (c) the appropriate length for the essay; (d) the use of test-taking strategies (i.e., *Use the* **ANSWER** *strategy to prepare your essay*); and (e) the point totals associated with essay questions.

students performed as a group and provides you and your students with a basis for comparing their test scores and learning to their classmates. You can use these data to see if your teaching was effective in helping your students learn the material and to identify students who need additional instruction.

When grading your students' tests, it is preferable to avoid using an X, slash, or a red-colored pen to mark incorrect answers as these indicators often have negative connotations for students. Therefore, you can use a more neutral symbol to note incorrect answers such as a question mark (?), place a checkmark next to the correct answer alternative in multiple-choice and true-false items, and write the correct words for sentence completion items and correct letters for matching items. Another alternative is to leave incorrect answers blank and to award points only for correct answers. You can write a rationale for your scoring that includes brief comments related to correct and incorrect parts of answers.

In addition to traditional ways of scoring tests, you can consider whether to use a variety of grading alternatives based on an analysis of your students' scores and your test items. These types of testing accommodations, which should be used cautiously and only occasionally to motivate your students and to reinforce their efforts to succeed on your tests, are presented in Chapter 2.

Keys to Best Practice: Establish an appropriate passing standard (National Board of Medical Examiners, 2002).

Establishing a Passing Standard

Prior to grading your tests, you should set a *passing standard,* which guides you in determining students' mastery levels and grades. There are two types of passing standards: *relative* and *absolute.* A *relative standard,* which is associated with grading on a curve, is a system where passing and failing are defined in terms of how a student does in comparison to the performance of others taking the test. Thus, if a teacher specifies that students scoring in the top 70% of the class pass and students scoring in the bottom 30% fail, the actual passing score would be adjusted based on the performance of the students taking the test. If students do very well on the test, the passing score will be raised to delineate the top 70% who pass, and if students perform poorly on the test, the passing score will be curved downward to identify the top 70% who pass the test.

Under an *absolute standard,* passing and failing is based on whether or not an individual student's test performance exceeds a minimum level of mastery you have established. For example, you might establish that a score of 65% or above is passing. Therefore, all students whose test scores are at least 65% have passed the test, and all students whose test scores are below 65% are considered as failing the test.

Generally, it is recommended that you use an absolute standard for your teacher-made tests. You would only consider using a relative standard if you needed to use the results of your test to determine awards, honors, or privileges that were available only to a limited number of your students. Whereas a relative standard can cause division and competition among students, using an absolute standard gives all of your students, including those with special needs, an opportunity to pass your tests based on their own performance. However, when using an absolute standard, it is critical that you establish a valid and fair level that compares student performance to an appropriate level of mastery in relation to your curriculum. Many teachers use absolute passing standards that parallel the levels used to judge passing on statewide and districtwide tests.

Keys to Best Practice: Perform an item analysis and use this information to revise your grading and your tests and to inform your instruction (Brookhart & Nitko, 2008; Hogan, 2007; National Board of Medical Examiners, 2002).

Performing an Item Analysis

Your grading should provide you with information to perform an *item analysis.* An item analysis is a process of examining your students' responses to individual test items to assess the extent to which the items are meeting your testing and instructional goals. By performing an item analysis you, like Ms. Dodd, can identify which of your items are too difficult or too simple for your students as well as which questions they find tricky, vague, or confusing. You can then use this information to validate effective and well-written test items, to revise or eliminate problematic items, to make changes in your scoring key, and to adjust your grading accordingly.

As part of your item analysis, you can examine each item to identify the specific content and skills assessed. This information can then be used to inform your instruction so that you can make changes in your teaching for students who need additional instruction.

You perform an item analysis by looking at each item to identify its level of difficulty, which is determined by the proportion of your students who answered it correctly. Item analysis and spreadsheet program software are available to help you conduct an item analysis (see Figure 1.1). You can then determine if the level of difficulty of each item is appropriate. This is an individual decision based on comparison of each item's level of difficulty with the learning goals your test assesses. Thus, rather than eliminating or revising items that the majority of your students answer correctly or incorrectly, you should make sure the item is a valid, accurate, important, and useful measure of the content you have taught.

An important part of an item analysis is examining your students' incorrect responses to see if there are common error patterns associated with the ways students answered a test item. You can then use this information to determine if a test item was confusing, inappropriate content-wise, in need of revision for some other reason, and whether you need to modify your instruction. For example, when performing an analysis of multiple-choice items, you can look at what percentage of your students selected each response choice and revise your answer options so that you

- replace response choices that students do not select;
- revise incorrect response choices that are selected as often as the correct answer, as this may indicate that the incorrect answer choice is misleading; and
- assess the usefulness of items where students' incorrect answers are evenly distributed among the different incorrect response choices, as this pattern may indicate that students are guessing. If this is the case, consider revising or eliminating the item and decide whether you need to modify the instruction you provided relative to the content assessed by the item (Brookhart & Nitko, 2008).

You can identify problematic items by asking students to explain why they selected a response or answered the way they did. You can ask them to think aloud and describe the thought process they used to approach a test question.

Keys to Best Practice: Observe your students during testing (Brookhart & Nitko, 2008; Hogan, 2007).

Observing Students

Observing your students while they are taking the test can provide you with information to support your item analysis and help you determine if your test is an accurate measure of their abilities. As Ms. Dodd did, you can observe your students' approach to testing tasks and use of test-taking skills and note their effort and attitude, organizational and attention skills, and frustration and anxiety levels. Generally, you want to determine if your students' behaviors were consistent throughout the testing, or whether their behaviors changed based on specific items or the length of time.

Keys to Best Practice: Provide feedback to students on their test performance and solicit feedback on your tests from them (Brookhart & Nitko, 2008; Hogan, 2007).

Providing and Soliciting Feedback

In addition to sharing their numerical grades with students, you can provide feedback to your students on their test performance. To help them understand their performance in relation to the class, you can share the class's mean, median, mode, and range with them. It is a good practice to provide individual students with comments on aspects of specific answers. These comments can help your students focus on their learning progress as well as the things they need to do to improve their performance on future tests. When students' answers are correct, your feedback can focus on their *content mastery* ("From this answer, I can see you understand the difference between similes and metaphors"), *effort* ("This answer shows you worked really hard on learning this"), and *use of effective test-taking strategies* ("You did a good job of using the ANSWER strategy"). When students' responses are incorrect, you can provide them with informational and strategy feedback ("You seemed to confuse these terms. I'm going to teach you another way to remember this information"). You also can use technology-based testing to provide your students with informational and immediate feedback regarding their test performance (see Chapter 3) and to provide students with feedback on their use of effective studying and test-taking skills strategies (we will learn more about these in Chapter 4).

After grading the test, you can review it with your class. You can lead your students in performing an item analysis to identify mastered and nonmastered items and content and the types of errors that were made. You can ask them why specific content was not mastered, why errors occurred, and what can be done to address these issues in the future.

As Ms. Dodd did with her students, you can solicit feedback from your students on all aspects of your tests. You can ask them to share their perspectives regarding important aspects of the test. For example, you can ask them the following questions:

- What did you think of the test?
- Were the test's directions and items clear?
- Did you have enough time to finish the test?
- Were any of the directions and items confusing? If so, what confused you?
- Did any of the test items surprise you? If so, which ones? Why were you surprised?
- Did any parts of the test frustrate you? If so, what parts? Why were they frustrating to you?
- How could I revise the test to improve it and make it fairer?

Students can reflect upon and provide feedback about their test performance. After reviewing their test performance, you can ask your students to respond to the following:

- The things I liked best about the test were _____.
- The things I didn't like about the test were _____.
- I was good at _____.
- I struggled with _____.
- The easiest parts of the test were _____.
- The hardest parts of the test were _____.
- The things that surprised me the most about my performance on the test were _____.
- The things that frustrated me the most about my performance on the test were _____.
- I would feel more comfortable during the test if I could _____.
- After taking this test, I realize I need to work on _____.

As Ms. Dodd did, you can use feedback from students in several ways to improve your tests. You can use their feedback as well as their error patterns to guide you in modifying your scoring key, creating upcoming tests, determining the need for grading alternatives, and preparing students for future tests. For example, if student feedback and test performance revealed that they experienced problems with matching items, you can examine your writing of these types of items, use other types of items, and provide them with some instruction on test-taking strategies for answering matching questions (see Chapter 4).

SUMMARY

This chapter provided best practices you can use to create and grade valid and accessible teacher-made tests. You also can use these practices to evaluate and revise the premade tests you receive from publishers of textbooks and other commercially produced instructional materials. You can use the reflectlist (see Figure 1.7) to review the main points presented in this chapter and to examine the extent to which you are applying best practices to create and grade valid and accessible teacher-made tests.

Figure 1.7 Reflectlist for Creating and Grading Valid and Accessible Teacher-Made Tests

Reflect on your ability to create and grade valid and accessible teacher-made tests by rating the extent to which you are applying the following keys to best practices.

Keys to Best Practice	Often	Sometimes	Rarely	Never
The content of my tests reflects my curriculum and assesses the most important topics, concepts, and skills I have taught.	☐	☐	☐	☐
The content of my tests is consistent with the instructional strategies I used to help my students learn.	☐	☐	☐	☐
I weight important and difficult topics more heavily on my tests.	☐	☐	☐	☐
I give frequent tests that assess specific content.	☐	☐	☐	☐
I involve students in determining the content of my tests.	☐	☐	☐	☐
I foster the readability of my tests by carefully paying attention to the language and the types and number of words and sentence structures I use.	☐	☐	☐	☐
I use software programs to make sure that the readability of my tests is appropriate for my students.	☐	☐	☐	☐
My tests pair text with visual supports.	☐	☐	☐	☐
I apply the principles of typographic and visual design to create legible and organized tests.	☐	☐	☐	☐
I format my tests to help students stay organized and pay attention.	☐	☐	☐	☐
I provide my students with strategy prompts and reminders.	☐	☐	☐	☐
I provide students with encouragement and motivation prompts and reminders.	☐	☐	☐	☐
I clearly introduce important aspects of my tests.	☐	☐	☐	☐
I carefully phrase and present directions for test items.	☐	☐	☐	☐
I use technology to help my students focus on and pay attention to test directions.	☐	☐	☐	☐

Keys to Best Practice	Often	Sometimes	Rarely	Never
When appropriate, I match the content and format of my test questions to the high-stakes tests my students will take.	☐	☐	☐	☐
My test questions are motivating, creative, challenging, and relevant to my students' lives and academic abilities.	☐	☐	☐	☐
My test questions are respectful and reflective of my students' individual differences.	☐	☐	☐	☐
I use effective guidelines for composing multiple-choice items.	☐	☐	☐	☐
I use effective guidelines for composing matching items.	☐	☐	☐	☐
I use effective guidelines for composing true-false items.	☐	☐	☐	☐
I use effective guidelines for composing sentence completion items.	☐	☐	☐	☐
I use effective guidelines for composing essay questions.	☐	☐	☐	☐
I create and use a complete scoring key or answer sheet.	☐	☐	☐	☐
I obtain raw scores and percentages.	☐	☐	☐	☐
I determine the mean, mode, median, and range for my students' test scores.	☐	☐	☐	☐
I establish an appropriate passing standard.	☐	☐	☐	☐
I perform an item analysis.	☐	☐	☐	☐
I observe my students during testing.	☐	☐	☐	☐
I provide feedback to students on their test performance.	☐	☐	☐	☐
I solicit feedback on my tests from students.	☐	☐	☐	☐
I use student performance and item analysis data and feedback from students to revise my grading and tests, and to inform my instruction.	☐	☐	☐	☐

- How would you rate your ability to create and grade valid and accessible teacher-made tests?
- What aspects are your strengths?
- In what areas do you need to improve?
- What steps can you take to improve your tests?

COMING ATTRACTIONS

As you use teacher-made tests, remember that student performance on tests is only one way to assess their learning and determine their report card grades. Keep in mind that teacher-made tests are limited in that test scores tend to be based on the quality of your tests and reflect only one score on a particular day under certain conditions. Therefore, in addition to using the best practices for creating and grading teacher-made tests presented in this chapter, you can strive to obtain a complete picture of student performance and enhance the effectiveness and inclusiveness of your teaching, testing, and assessment practices by

- determining and implementing valid and appropriate testing accommodations for use by your students who need them (see Chapter 2);
- using technology-based testing (see Chapter 3);
- teaching effective study and test-taking skills and strategies to your students (see Chapter 4); and
- using classroom assessments (see Chapter 5).

2

Determining and Implementing Valid and Appropriate Testing Accommodations

I know I need testing accommodations to pass and graduate. I think they help me show others what I have learned. But some of them are unnecessary and embarrassing. Sometimes the person giving me the test gives me hints I don't need. I hate it when they make me leave the classroom to take a test. It makes me feel different, and the other kids always ask me why I have to leave.

—A student with a disability

Although I understand the need for some testing accommodations, some of them are inappropriate and unfair. They change the nature of my tests and give students with disabilities an advantage over other students. I wish they would consult me and consider the other students when making decisions about testing accommodations.

—A general education teacher

I was very disappointed, confused, and angry. I worked with the IEP team to identify the testing accommodations my son should receive. We listed them in the IEP and I assumed he would receive them, especially for the state tests. Then they told me the state says he can use only state-approved testing accommodations when taking the state tests. What about the other testing accommodations he's supposed to receive? He uses them to take his teachers' tests. Why can't he use them for the state tests?

—A parent of a student with a disability

Some of our students' families are very savvy. They are used to getting what they want, and many of them want their children to have the advantage of having testing accommodations when they take tests to improve their chances of getting into college.

—A special education teacher

(Continued)

(Continued)

Although it has caused us to focus more on students with diverse and special needs, NCLB places an overreliance on standardized testing and forces schools to adopt a one-size-fits-all approach. The judging of a school's success at making adequate yearly progress based on the results of standardized tests for different groups of students with special needs can make these students scapegoats, particularly students with disabilities. Testing accommodations related to IDEIA help us level the playing field for some of our students with special needs, and many of them are testing quite well. Unfortunately, many are falling farther behind.

—A school administrator

- What concerns do these individuals have about testing accommodations?
- What have been your experiences with testing accommodations?
- How would you and your school address these concerns?

As these comments indicate, there are many issues in determining and implementing appropriate testing accommodations (see Figure 2.1). Often these issues are interconnected and present challenges when deciding which of your students should receive testing accommodations, and in selecting and implementing valid testing accommodations for the different types of tests your students take (Ketterlin-Geller, Alonzo et al., 2007). This chapter helps you overcome these challenges by offering a variety of best practices you and your colleagues can use to determine and implement valid and appropriate testing accommodations for your students. Specifically, this chapter addresses the following questions:

- What are the elements of valid testing accommodations?
- What are the different types of testing accommodations?
- Who is eligible to receive testing accommodations?
- How are valid and appropriate testing accommodations for students determined?
- How can the implementation of testing accommodations be fostered?

Figure 2.1   Issues Related to Testing Accommodations

- Complying with NCLB and IDEIA
- Understanding what makes up valid testing accommodations
- Distinguishing between high-stakes and teacher-made testing
- Deciding who receives which testing accommodations
- Having a process for making decisions regarding testing accommodations
- Ensuring the implementation of identified testing accommodations
- Dealing with issues of fairness, appropriateness, and effectiveness
- Considering the acceptability (stigma) of testing accommodations

Source: From "Determining Appropriate Testing Accommodations: Complying With NCLB and IDEA," by S. J. Salend, *Teaching Exceptional Children, 40*(4), 2008, p. 15. Copyright © 2008 by the Council for Exceptional Children. Reprinted with permission.

Keys to Best Practice: Understand that valid testing accommodations should provide your students with access to tests without altering the content, constructs, or results of your tests or giving students an advantage over their classmates (Byrnes, 2008; Cox, Herner, Demczyk, & Nieberding, 2006; Edgemon, Jablonski, & Lloyd, 2006).

WHAT ARE THE ELEMENTS OF VALID TESTING ACCOMMODATIONS?

As some of the comments at the beginning of this chapter suggest, what makes a valid testing accommodation is often misunderstood. Valid testing accommodations are changes in the testing administration, environment, equipment, technology, and procedures that allow students to participate in testing programs and do not change the nature of the test (Byrnes, 2008; Cox et al., 2006; Edgemon et al., 2006). Valid testing accommodations are designed to provide students with access to tests without altering the tests or giving students an advantage over others. For example, having a proctor read test items would not be a valid testing accommodation on a reading test as it changes the nature of the test from reading to listening comprehension. However, it might be an appropriate testing accommodation for use on a mathematics test that is not designed to assess reading. Therefore, whether your students are taking state, districtwide, or teacher-made tests, an essential element defining a valid testing accommodation is that it must not change the test's content, constructs, and results.

WHAT ARE THE DIFFERENT TYPES OF TESTING ACCOMMODATIONS?

Because of the varied purposes of testing and the unique qualities of your students, it is important for you to be aware of a range of possible testing accommodations. Testing accommodations are usually categorized as relating to presentation and response mode formats; to timing, scheduling, and setting alternatives and to linguistically based factors (Salend, 2008). A range of possible testing accommodations is presented in Figure 2.2.

Many educators also consider grading alternatives and instruction to improve students' study skills as well as their test-taking strategies to be types of testing accommodation (we will discuss ways in which you can teach your students how to study and take tests in Chapter 4).

Recent advances in technology-based testing are offering new ways to design and implement all types of testing accommodations (Ketterlin-Geller, Yovanoff, & Tindal, 2007). Thus, technology provides alternatives to traditional testing formats and allows for the implementation of customized testing accommodations for individual students (we will discuss technology-based testing in Chapter 3).

Keys to Best Practice: Be aware of a range of presentation mode testing accommodations (Clapper, Morse, Thurlow, & Thompson, 2006; Edgemon et al., 2006; Elbaum, 2007).

Figure 2.2   Possible Testing Accommodations

(a) PRESENTATION MODE ACCOMMODATIONS

- Reading directions and items aloud
- Clarifying or simplifying language
- Repeating directions as necessary
- Listing directions in sequential order
- Increasing the spacing between items
- Highlighting changes in the directions
- Presenting only one sentence per line
- Using markers or masks to maintain place
- Using reminders
- Highlighting *key* words or phrases
- Organizing or sequencing items appropriately and logically
- Providing a sample of each item type
- Placing fewer items on a page
- Providing a proctor
- Offering aid in turning pages and maintaining place
- Presenting tests via signing or Braille

(b) RESPONSE MODE ACCOMMODATIONS

- Responding via native language or preferred mode of communication
- Providing extra space
- Using lined or grid paper
- Using enlarged answer bubbles or blocks
- Providing check sheets, graphic organizers, and outlines
- Providing a proctor to monitor place and the recording of answers
- Answering on the test
- Allowing students to dictate answers
- Fewer items per page
- Using multiple-choice items
- Giving oral exams, open-book tests, and take home tests
- Providing a scribe

(c) TIMING AND SCHEDULING ACCOMMODATIONS

- Giving more time or untimed tests
- Providing shorter versions of tests
- Allowing breaks as needed
- Adjusting the testing order
- Eliminating items or sections
- Varying the times of the testing sessions
- Scheduling shorter testing sessions
- Administering tests over several days

(d) TIMING, SCHEDULING, AND SETTING ACCOMMODATIONS

- Taking tests in small groups or individually in separate locations
- Allowing movement and background sounds
- Providing preferential seating arrangements (carrels)
- Providing adaptive furniture or equipment
- Eliminating visual and auditory distractions
- Delivering reinforcement
- Providing specific environmental arrangements (lighting, acoustics, sound amplification)

(e) LINGUISTICALLY BASED ACCOMMODATIONS

- Using understandable and familiar language
- Repeating orally based directions or items
- Teaching the language of academic testing
- Pairing items or directions with graphics or pictures
- Translating tests
- Allowing responses in native languages or dialects
- Offering review sheets and lists of important vocabulary
- Allowing use of bilingual materials (bilingual glossaries or dictionaries)
- Providing context clues
- Providing alternate ways to demonstrate mastery of test material
- Providing translators to administer tests

Source: From "Determining Appropriate Testing Accommodations: Complying With NCLB and IDEA," by S. J. Salend, *Teaching Exceptional Children, 40*(4), 2008, p. 17. Copyright © 2008 by the Council for Exceptional Children. Reprinted with permission.

Presentation Mode Testing Accommodations

Presentation mode testing accommodations involve changes in the ways test questions and directions are presented to your students. Possible presentation mode testing accommodations are presented in Figure 2.2(a).

One very popular presentation mode accommodation is having an educator read aloud the test's directions and items to students who experience difficulty reading text (Elbaum, 2007). Readers can improve their effectiveness and ensure the integrity of the test by following the guidelines presented in Figure 2.3 (many of these guidelines also are appropriate for scribes, proctors, translators, and interpreters).

Figure 2.3   Guidelines for Reading Tests to Students

Prior to the Test Administration

- Read and review the test and learn the definitions and pronunciations of unfamiliar terms and mathematical and scientific expressions and formulas
- Eliminate generic directions if they are not appropriate for the testing situation
- Make sure that testing materials are organized and presented in a way that makes it easy for you to access and follow
- Review testing materials to understand all of the administration conditions associated with the test (i.e., allowable and prohibited test administration actions)
- Distribute testing materials to students in accordance with the test's directions

During the Test Administration

- Refrain from alerting students to their errors and confirming correct responses
- Avoid providing assistance, cueing, and engaging in actions that impact the student's answers such as

  o Reminding, prompting, coaching, and teaching students
  o Unnecessarily highlighting or paraphrasing important information
  o Changing your voice
  o Explaining vocabulary, concepts, and visuals
  o Clarifying and elaborating on parts of the test

- Read only approved parts of the test (e.g., reading passages and questions assessing reading comprehension can impact the validity of those items by making them into measures of listening comprehension)
- Read all of the text on the test including directions, examples, and items
- Establish an appropriate pace that includes reading all parts of the question before soliciting and acknowledging the student's answer(s)
- Reread the entire question when asked to repeat a question to make sure that critical parts of questions are not inadvertently highlighted
- Consider facilitating the validity of the test administration and the rereading process by making a digital recording of the test administration (e.g., replaying questions that have been asked to be repeated)
- Use your voice to highlight key parts of questions that are printed in boldface, italics, or capitals
- Spell synonyms and other words requested by the student (if permissible)
- Redirect off-task comments from the student
- Observe students for signs of fatigue as reading tests tends to make the testing experience longer and more tiring

---

Source: Adapted from Clapper, Morse, Thurlow, & Thompson (2006).

Test Proctors

Some students will require the assistance of a proctor (Cox et al., 2006). In the case of deaf or hard-of-hearing students, the proctor should be a professional who can sign and interpret oral directions and translate their answers (Clapper et al., 2006). Proctors can help students take tests by

- reading, repeating, or simplifying the test directions and items;
- adjusting the pace at which the test is administered;
- noticing when students tire and modifying the testing schedule and administration accordingly;
- responding to student questions about the test;
- turning pages for students who have motor difficulties;
- assisting students in maintaining their place; and
- prompting students to pay attention and sustain their effort.

Like readers, scribes, interpreters, and translators, proctors should be careful not to give students cues, hints, and additional information that may affect their answers.

Keys to Best Practice: Be aware of a range of response mode testing accommodations (Byrnes, 2008; Clapper et al., 2006; Cox et al., 2006; Edgemon et al., 2006).

Response Mode Testing Accommodations

Response mode testing accommodations refer to changes in the way students are asked to respond to test items or determine their answers. Possible response mode testing accommodations are presented in Figure 2.2(b).

Accommodations for Students With Writing and Speaking Difficulties

Since most tests require written or oral responses, your students with writing and speaking difficulties may particularly benefit from adjustments in the ways that they can respond to test items. To minimize difficulty in transferring responses to separate answer sheets, you can have students

- mark their responses on the test protocol,
- use enlarged answer bubbles, or
- fold test pages and position the answer sheet so that only one page appears at a time.

In addition to giving oral answers in lieu of written responses, your students with writing difficulties can be given tests that are formatted to

- contain fewer items per page,
- provide extra space between items,
- present items on lined or grid paper,
- have a larger space in which to write test answers, and
- use multiple-choice questions rather than essay items.

Your students with verbal difficulties can write or indicate their responses in alternative ways. For example, deaf and hard-of-hearing students can respond via sign language, and students with physical disabilities can respond through use of eye movements (Clapper et al., 2006).

Responding to Essay Questions

You can take several actions to try to make sure that writing difficulties do not severely impact your students' ability to demonstrate their mastery of the content being assessed on essay questions. You can provide these students with check sheets, graphic organizers, or outlines listing the components that can guide them in organizing their essays and make sure they have sufficient time to draft and write their answers. On essay questions where the focus is on content, students can be provided with graphics and resources that allow them to take notes and prepare responses to essay questions (Chapter 3 provides a range of technology students can use to answer essay questions). For example, when students are asked to compare concepts, you can provide them with an outline of a compare-and-contrast chart, and when students need to discuss the relationships between concepts, you can provide them with an outline of a semantic web.

When grammar, spelling, and punctuation are not important components in grading, students can dictate their responses into a digital audio recorder or take an oral exam. However, keep in mind that oral exams can be intimidating. To minimize anxiety, you can give students opportunities to practice responding orally and allow them to use visual aids and manipulatives to supplement their answers.

You can structure your administration of essay items by using alternate forms of essays such as open-book tests and take-home tests. During open-book tests, students are permitted to use their books and notes to answer essay questions. Take-home tests, which allow students to use a range of resources to complete essay questions, are good ways to motivate students to apply the important concepts and topics to problem-based essay questions. However, when using take-home tests, you need to establish rules and procedures that ensure that your students do not write excessively long responses and that they do not receive assistance from others.

Scribes

When appropriate, students can be asked to dictate their responses to a trained scribe. During testing, a trained scribe should

- establish that students, not scribes, are responsible for reading all parts of the question to themselves;
- make a verbatim record of students' dictated responses, beginning each sentence with a capital and ending each sentence with a period;
- keep their copy of the response hidden until students indicate that they are finished dictating their response;
- refrain from editing students' responses and questioning, correcting, and coaching students; and
- use index cards marked with letters or numbers to allow students to indicate their choices on objective tests such as multiple-choice and true-false questions (Clapper et al., 2006).

Scribes may want to make a digital recording of the session to ensure that student responses were written as dictated and that no assistance or prompting was provided to students.

When your students use a scribe, it is important for them to understand that they are responsible for reviewing their dictated verbatim responses in terms of formatting, grammar, punctuation, word choices, capitalization, and spelling of words than contain more than two letters, and to make or direct the scribe to make changes. Therefore, your students who use scribes should practice how to use the services of a scribe before taking tests. If the students' final responses are difficult to read or a response must be recorded in a test booklet, scribes may record the responses in the desired format.

Keys to Best Practice: Be aware of a range of timing, scheduling, and setting testing accommodations (Byrnes, 2008; Cohen, Gregg, & Deng, 2005; Elliott & Marquart, 2004).

Timing, Scheduling, and Setting Testing Accommodations

Some of your students may need timing, scheduling, and setting accommodations. These accommodations are particularly helpful when your students

- have problems with processing information and being on-task or motivated;
- require additional time to use specialized testing techniques (such as dictating answers or reading test items aloud);
- need specialized testing conditions (such as special lighting, acoustics, or equipment or furniture);
- have physical conditions that cause them to tire easily;
- experience test anxiety; and
- take medications that are effective only for a limited amount of time or have side effects that affect performance.

A range of possible timing and scheduling alternatives are available for your students who need them (see Figure 2.2[c]). Students can be given additional time or shorter versions of tests. The scheduling of tests also can be adjusted for your students by

- allowing them to take breaks more frequently,
- modifying the order in which specific parts of test(s) are administered,
- breaking the testing session into several shorter periods, and
- administering tests over several days or at times students are most likely to be productive.

A variety of setting alternatives also are available for your students. While some students may perform better when they take tests in a small group or individually in a quiet location free of distractions, other students may need to have preferential seating arrangements, to move around, or to have some type of background sounds. Your students with physical disabilities may require adaptive furniture or devices, and your students with sensory impairments and attention difficulties may need specific environmental arrangements, specialized lighting, acoustics, or sound-field amplification systems. Some students may need preferential seating so that they are near you, another adult, or a positive role model and in a nondistracting classroom location. Your students who need assistance in maintaining their motivation may benefit from a separate testing location that provides them with verbal praise or tangible and activity reinforcers and allows you or others to monitor their behavior and performance.

Keys to Best Practice: Be aware of a range of linguistically based testing accommodations (Albus, Thurlow, Liu, & Bielinski, 2005; Herrera, Murry, & Cabral, 2007).

Linguistically Based Testing Accommodations

In addition to the previously mentioned testing accommodations, several specialized linguistically based accommodations can be used when testing your students who are English language learners (see Figure 2.2[d]). Since language proficiency can affect students' test performance, you can foster comprehension of test items and directions by

- using familiar and easy-to-understand language,
- reading and repeating directions and items, and
- pairing items and directions with culturally appropriate pictures and graphics (Herrera et al., 2007).

You can allow your students who are English language learners to use individually designed simplified bilingual dictionaries, glossaries, and word lists. When using these types of materials, it is important for you to make sure that they provide only direct translations of words and do not offer definitions or explanations of key terms and concepts. You can allow these students to show mastery of test content in other ways, such as with projects completed by cooperative learning groups or via the use of drawings, charts, manipulatives, demonstrations, or drama (Albus et al., 2005).

Translation

When appropriate, your students who are English language learners can take translated and alternate language versions of tests, be provided with translators to administer tests, and be permitted to respond in their native language or dialect. However, it is important for you and your colleagues to realize that translation does not remove the bias that may exist in tests. Thus, if you give translated test items that include questions that do not relate to your students' learning and cultural experiences and developmental and language levels, they will still struggle to answer them correctly, whether they are answering in English or their native language.

Keys to Best Practice: Be aware of grading alternatives and use them cautiously and occasionally to motivate your students and reinforce their efforts to succeed on tests (Brookhart & Nitko, 2008; Salend & Garrick Duhaney, 2002; Stern & Avigliano, 2008).

Grading Alternatives

In addition to the accommodations during testing we just discussed, you can consider whether to use a variety of grading alternatives when scoring students' tests. These alternatives, which should be used cautiously and only occasionally to motivate all of your students and to reinforce their efforts to succeed on your tests, include the following:

- Eliminate certain items, especially those items that you and your students find confusing, tricky, or unnecessarily difficult.
- Award partial credit for aspects of answers that are correct and for showing correct work.
- Offer extra-credit opportunities. It is best to make extra credit an integral part of the test rather than making it an option after the test has been administered, because extra credit should not be used to help students compensate for poor test performance that is due to their lack of effort.
- Give bonus points for specific questions. Informing students that there are secret bonus point questions on tests can motivate students to give detailed and complete answers to all test questions.
- Allow students to earn back points by correcting incorrect answers using their notes and textbooks, or retaking test questions that they answered incorrectly.
- Deduct points for incorrect answers. Some teachers do this to discourage students from guessing and to prepare them for high-stakes tests that use similar scoring procedures.
- Adjust how you grade essay responses. When the mechanics of the written response are not the elements being tested, you can give students some credit for an outline, web, diagram, or chart in lieu of writing a lengthy response. You also can modify your penalties for writing errors or assign your students separate grades for content and mechanics. For example, if an essay response on a social studies or science test is correct in terms of the content but contains numerous misspelled words, you can give your student separate grades for content and spelling (Brookhart & Nitko, 2008; Salend & Garrick Duhaney, 2002; Stern & Avigliano, 2008).

These options can be used judiciously to motivate students periodically to expand their learning and demonstrate their mastery of concepts. When considering these options, be careful that you do not inadvertently excuse students from studying and preparing for tests. Some teachers set rules relating to the number of times students can use these options, the maximum grade a student can receive for a test that was originally below a certain level (e.g., grades on retakes cannot exceed 80%), and the types of items that cannot be retaken (e.g., extra-credit items cannot be retaken).

Giving Students Choices

Some teachers try to make their grading fairer by giving students choices (Salend, 2008). When using objective test items, consider giving students the option of writing a justification of their response to items for which they are unsure of the answer. You can then use their justification to award partial credit to students whose justifications make sense or to eliminate confusing test items.

You also can give students the opportunity to select the type of test they take. For example, you can organize your tests so they offer students choices in responding to items. Thus, a test can consist of 25 items with varying formats, and students can be directed to respond to any 15 of them in whatever format they choose. Those students who are proficient at multiple-choice items but who have difficulty with essay questions can select more of the former and fewer of the latter. Similarly, you can create several equivalent versions of a test such as a multiple-choice test, an essay test, an oral test, and a test containing a variety of items. Your students can then select the test version that best fits their strengths and challenges.

Cooperative Group Testing

Another alternative way to grade your tests is through *cooperative group testing* (Pomplun, 1996; Salend, 2008). Cooperative group testing involves having your students work collaboratively on open-ended problem-solving activities that typically have a variety of solutions. Each group of students creates one product, which reflects the contributions of all group members. You then grade this product, with each student in the group receiving the group grade. For example, to test students' mastery of material related to amphibians, students can work in groups to complete an open-ended test or an activity related to different amphibians.

When using cooperative group testing, concerns about the equitable contributions of each member of the group can be addressed in a variety of ways. You can have each group keep a log that lists the group's activities, including a summary of each group member's contribution and effort. As part of their grade, students can be randomly asked to respond individually to questions about their group's test.

You can employ a *two-tiered testing system* (Gajria, Giek, Hemrick, & Salend, 1992; Salend, 2008). This method involves students completing a test in collaborative groups, with each student receiving the group grade. Following the group test, students individually complete a second test that covers similar content. You can reverse the order of the tests and have students initially complete the test individually and then in a collaborative group with their classmates (Michaelson & Sweet, 2008). You can then choose to grade students by giving them a separate group and individual testing grade, averaging or weighting their group and individual grade together into one grade, or giving them the option of selecting their higher grade.

WHO IS ELIGIBLE TO RECEIVE TESTING ACCOMMODATIONS?

Keys to Best Practice: Work with the multidisciplinary team to determine if your students are eligible to receive testing accommodations under IDEIA or Section 504 and whether students should take general grade level assessments or alternate assessments (Byrnes, 2008; Edgemon et al., 2006; Ketterlin-Geller, Alonzo, et al., 2007; Towles-Reeves, Kleinert, & Muhomba, 2009).

Not all students are eligible to receive testing accommodations. Typically, your students who have been identified by a multidisciplinary team as having a disability under IDEIA or Section 504 are eligible to receive testing accommodations. There are four levels for assessing your students with disabilities under NCLB and IDEIA with the vast majority of them being tested at Levels 1 and 2 (see Figure 2.4).

Figure 2.4 Levels for Assessing Students With Disabilities Under NCLB and IDEIA

Level 1: General Education Assessments Without Testing Accommodations: At this level, your students with disabilities participate in high-stakes testing programs aligned with statewide learning standards by taking the same general grade-level assessments and teacher-made tests as their classmates without disabilities. Level 1 students typically

- require relatively few instructional accommodations to access the general education curriculum and
- are likely to achieve grade-level proficiency in the same time frame as their classmates without disabilities.

Level 2: General Education Assessments With Testing Accommodations: At this level, your students with disabilities take the same general grade-level assessments and teacher-made tests as their classmates without disabilities but with testing accommodations. Level 2 students have many of the same characteristics as Level 1 students. However, they typically require you and their other teachers to implement more instructional accommodations to help them access and master the general education curriculum in a time frame that closely resembles their peers.

Level 3: Alternate Assessments Based on Modified Academic Standards: Rather than taking the general education assessments and teacher-made tests that their classmates take, Level 3 students take alternate assessments based on *modified academic achievement standards.* These modified academic achievement standards address challenging but less difficult grade-level content from the general education curriculum. For example, Level 3 students might take less rigorous grade-level content tests that have multiple-choice items with fewer choices or reading tests that ask them to read fewer passages. These modified standards and alternate assessments are designed for use with your students with disabilities who

- do not have a significant cognitive disability,
- have access to grade-level content instruction,
- have IEPs that include goals addressing grade-level content standards, and
- are not likely to reach grade-level proficiency in the same time frame as their classmates without disabilities.

Level 4: Modified Assessments Based on Alternate Achievement Standards: Level 4 students take modified assessments that relate to *alternate achievement standards* that are not as complex as the state's grade level achievement standards or your teacher-made tests. The modified assessments include work samples and the collection and documentation of products of student learning via teacher observation. They may take the form of audio and video digital recordings of students performing various activities related to alternate achievement standards. In most states, these collections of student work are linked to statewide standards and evaluated via performance assessment, portfolios, or through use of a checklist or an instructional rubric (we will learn more about these types of assessments in Chapter 5). These modified assessments are designed for your students with significant cognitive disabilities who

- take a class for reasons other than mastery of the general education curriculum,
- require extensive instructional modifications, and
- are not able to participate in high-stakes testing even with testing accommodations.

Once your individual students are identified as eligible for testing accommodations, you and your colleagues can use the following guidelines to determine which testing accommodations are valid and appropriate for them.

HOW ARE VALID AND APPROPRIATE TESTING ACCOMMODATIONS FOR STUDENTS DETERMINED?

Keys to Best Practice: Decisions regarding the use of specific testing accommodations should be determined individually for your students based on their unique characteristics and learning strengths and challenges (Byrnes, 2008; Brinckerhoff & Banerjee, 2007; Edgemon et al., 2006).

Rather than being disability based, decisions regarding the use of specific testing accommodations should be determined individually for your students and related to information about their unique characteristics and learning strengths

Figure 2.5   Resources for Selecting and Implementing Testing Accommodations

1. National Center on Educational Outcomes Special Topic Area: Accommodations for Students with Disabilities (www.cehd.umn.edu/nceo/TopicAreas/Accommodations/StatesAccomm.htm)
2. *How to develop state guidelines for access assistants: Scribes, readers, and sign language interpreters* (Clapper et al., 2006).
3. *Survey of teacher recommendations for accommodation* (Ketterlin-Geller, Alonzo et al., 2007).
4. *The assessment accommodation checklist* (Elliott, Kratochwill, & Schulte, 1998).
5. *Dynamic assessment of test accommodations* (Fuchs & Fuchs, 2001).

and challenges (Brinckerhoff & Banerjee, 2007; Byrnes, 2008). This means that testing accommodations for your students with disabilities should be based on each student's characteristics so that the testing accommodations

- match the instructional accommodations that support student learning,
- comply with state and districtwide policies, and
- are responsive to the perspectives of students and teachers.

It is important to be aware that your students may benefit from more than one testing accommodation and may therefore need packages of different types of testing accommodations (Edgemon et al., 2006). Resources to assist you and your colleagues in selecting testing accommodations for students with a wide range of disabilities are presented in Figure 2.5.

Keys to Best Practice: Testing accommodations should match the effective instructional accommodations regularly used by students in their daily classroom instruction (Cox et al., 2006; Ketterlin-Geller, Alonzo, et al., 2007).

Matching Testing Accommodations to Effective Teaching Accommodations

Your students' testing accommodations should match the effective teaching accommodations you use within your daily classroom instruction to support student learning. For instance, the instructional accommodation you use to help a student understand classroom directions also should be used to help the student understand test directions and items. You can use the following questions to gather information about your students and the teaching accommodations that support their learning:

- Does the student have sensory, medical, physical, or attention conditions that affect classroom performance? If so, what are these conditions and what strategies and resources are used to address them?
- Does the student exhibit academic and social behaviors that interfere with learning or the learning of others? If so, what are these behaviors and what strategies, classroom arrangements, resources, and technologies are used to address them?

- What instructional methods, approaches, strategies, specialized equipment, technology, materials, or classroom designs have been successful in supporting the student's learning?
- What instructional strategies, resources, and technologies are used to help the student understand directions and respond to classroom activities?
- What are the student's learning and testing style preferences?
- What instructional strategies, resources, and technologies are used to help students complete assignments?
- Does the student need additional time or motivation to complete assignments?

Keys to Best Practice: Comply with statewide and districtwide policies regarding testing accommodations (Byrnes, 2008; Cox et al., 2006; Elliott & Thurlow, 2006; Ketterlin-Geller, Alonzo, et al., 2007).

Keys to Best Practice: Differentiate between testing accommodations that are appropriate for high-stakes assessments and teacher-made tests and make these distinctions explicit via your students' IEPs and 504 accommodation plans (Byrnes, 2008; Salend, 2008).

Complying With Statewide and Districtwide Policies and Differentiating Between High-Stakes Assessments and Teacher-Made Tests

The types of testing accommodations used by your students will depend on your state's and district's policies and the types of tests they will be taking. This means that the testing accommodations available for use by your students will be guided by whether they are taking high-stakes assessments or teacher-made tests.

Testing Accommodations and High-Stakes Testing

In the case of students who need testing accommodations to participate in high-stakes assessment, it is essential to comply with state and districtwide policies regarding approved accommodations. In making these determinations, states consider whether the accommodation is appropriate and valid and would provide access by eliminating or lessening difficulties related to disability or second language acquisition without altering the test or providing an advantage over other test takers. Therefore, testing accommodations selected for use on high-stakes tests must be consistent with state and districtwide policies and must be provided under certain testing situations (Elliott & Thurlow, 2006). For instance, some states mandate that a testing accommodation be employed for a specific period of time in classroom instruction before it can be used during high-stakes testing. Some states also have provisions whereby multidisciplinary teams can seek permission from their state's department of education to allow individual students to use accommodations that are not listed as approved. Since accommodations allowed in one state may not be allowed in other states and policies vary from state to state, you and your colleagues should obtain information about your state's testing accommodations policies by contacting your state education department or visiting its Web site.

Testing Accommodations and Districtwide and Teacher-Made Testing

Although testing accommodations on statewide tests are determined by individual states, selections regarding appropriate testing accommodations for your classroom tests are made by you and your colleagues on multidisciplinary teams. Therefore, there is typically more flexibility when selecting testing accommodations for use by your students when they take districtwide and teacher-made tests. For example, while use of a thesaurus for a high-stakes statewide writing test may not be approved, you and your colleagues on the multidisciplinary team may determine that it is an appropriate testing accommodation for teacher-made tests in a range of content area classes. However, even when students are taking teacher-made and districtwide tests, testing accommodations should provide access without altering the test or giving students an advantage on the test. Keep in mind that there also may be districtwide testing policies that must be followed. To avoid the confusion, disappointment, and anger experienced by the parent at the beginning of this chapter, it is important to differentiate among testing accommodations that are used during the administration of state, districtwide, and teacher-made tests. It is essential to make these distinctions very clear to everyone, especially students and their families, by listing them on students' IEPs or 504 accommodation plans.

Keys to Best Practice: Make efforts to match testing accommodations used by students for teacher-made tests with those allowed for high-stakes tests so that students can become more familiar with the conditions they will encounter when taking high-stakes tests (Salend, 2008).

For most students, it is beneficial for the testing accommodations used for teacher-made tests and high-stakes tests to match each other. That way, students can become more familiar with the conditions they will encounter when taking high-stakes tests, and you can assess student performance with respect to how students are tested on high-stakes assessments.

Keys to Best Practice: Consider the perspectives of your students when selecting testing accommodations for them, including whether testing accommodations are fair, age appropriate, and do not adversely affect students or their classmates (Edgemon et al., 2006; Elliott & Marquart, 2004; Salend, 2008).

Considering the Perspectives of Students

Another important factor to consider when selecting testing accommodations is how specific accommodations are viewed by students. In terms of your students, it is important to make sure that testing accommodations are fair and do not adversely affect your students who receive them or their classmates. For example, many students might feel similar to the student quoted at the beginning of this chapter who felt that taking tests in separate locations was embarrassing, isolating, and stigmatizing. Additionally, it is essential that the testing accommodations you use with your students with disabilities are age appropriate.

Keys to Best Practice: Testing accommodations selected for students with disabilities should boost their performance and have a limited impact on the performance of their classmates (Bouck & Bouck, 2008; Fuchs & Fuchs, 2001).

It is important that testing accommodations selected for your students with disabilities give them a *differential boost* (Fuchs & Fuchs, 2001). In other words, the testing accommodations selected for your students with disabilities should boost their performance and, if used by their classmates, should have little positive effect on their classmates' test performance (Bouck & Bouck, 2008). For example, while having items read aloud can help students with reading difficulties, other students may find that it makes some test items more difficult and causes the testing session to be longer. If a testing accommodation benefits both your students with and without disabilities, you need to be careful to make sure it is not changing the nature of your test.

Keys to Best Practice: Consider the perspectives of teachers when selecting testing accommodations, including whether testing accommodations are valid, effective, easy to use, appropriate for the setting and student, and reasonable and whether they impact the integrity of tests (Cox et al., 2006; Edgemon et al., 2006; Elliott & Marquart, 2004).

Considering the Perspectives of Teachers

You and your colleagues' perspectives need to be considered when selecting testing accommodations. Therefore, when selecting possible testing accommodations for use with your students, you and your colleagues need to reflect on whether they are valid, effective, and appropriate by assessing whether and how specific accommodations affect the integrity of the tests and their administration. In addition, viewpoints about ease of implementation and reasonableness of specific testing accommodations should be examined by considering the extent to which you and your colleagues have the materials, time, resources, education, technology, and equipment needed to implement the testing accommodations.

HOW CAN THE IMPLEMENTATION OF TESTING ACCOMMODATIONS BE FOSTERED?

Keys to Best Practice: Foster implementation of the testing accommodations via students' IEPs and 504 accommodations plans including listing whether testing accommodations are appropriate for state, districtwide, and classroom testing, and the individuals, roles, resources, and preparation needed for implementation (Byrnes, 2008; Cox et al., 2006; MacArthur & Cavalier, 2004; Salend, 2008).

As we saw in several of the comments at the beginning of this chapter, there are times when testing accommodations are implemented inappropriately or unnecessarily. Therefore, you and your colleagues should consider the factors that foster implementation of testing accommodations by listing on IEPs and 504 accommodation plans

- which testing accommodations are appropriate for state, districtwide, and classroom testing;
- how these testing accommodations will be implemented;
- which individuals will be responsible for implementing the testing accommodations;
- what resources (materials, technology, locations, and equipment) will be needed to implement the testing accommodations; and

- what preparation will students and educators need to implement the testing accommodations (Byrnes, 2008; Cox et al., 2006; MacArthur & Cavalier, 2004; Salend, 2008).

For instance, while using a scribe can be an effective testing accommodation, many students may need instruction to teach them how to dictate to a scribe effectively. Similarly, educators who will serve as scribes, readers, proctors, and translators should be taught how to perform their roles effectively and appropriately (see Figure 2.3) and how to avoid giving students cues and additional information that may affect answers.

Keys to Best Practice: Evaluate your students' testing accommodations, and use this information to determine whether testing accommodations should be continued, revised, discontinued, or gradually faded out (Cox et al., 2006; Edgemon et al., 2006; Ketterlin-Geller, Alonzo, et al., 2007).

You can ensure the successful implementation of testing accommodations by using the guidelines presented in the introduction for continually evaluating them in terms of their validity, effectiveness, efficiency, fairness, and impact on you and your students. Effective testing accommodations can be continued if necessary, or gradually faded out so that your students with special needs take tests in the same ways as their classmates if possible. Similarly, efforts should be made to make sure that effective testing accommodations used for teacher-made tests match those allowed for high-stakes tests so that students can become more familiar with the conditions they will encounter when taking high-stakes tests. Testing accommodations that are not achieving their intended outcomes should be revised to make them more effective or discontinued.

SUMMARY

This chapter provided best practices for determining and implementing valid and appropriate testing accommodations for your students. These best practices allow you to respond to the many challenges you, your colleagues, your students, and their families face in responding to the testing mandates of NCLB and IDEIA. You can use the reflectlist (see Figure 2.6) to review the main points presented in this chapter and to examine the extent to which you and your colleagues are applying best practices to determine and implement valid and appropriate testing accommodations for your students.

COMING ATTRACTIONS

In addition to creating and grading valid and accessible teacher-made tests (see Chapter 1) and using the best practices presented in this chapter, you can enhance the effectiveness and inclusiveness of your teaching, testing, and assessment practices by

- using technology-based testing with your students (see Chapter 3),
- teaching effective study and test-taking skills and strategies to your students (see Chapter 4), and
- using classroom assessment to supplement your testing (see Chapter 5).

Figure 2.6   Reflectlist for Determining and Implementing Valid and Appropriate Testing Accommodations for Students

Reflect on your ability to determine and implement valid and appropriate testing accommodations for your students by rating the extent to which you are applying the following keys to best practices.

Keys to Best Practice	Often	Sometimes	Rarely	Never
I work with the multidisciplinary team to determine if my students are eligible to receive testing accommodations under IDEIA or Section 504.	☐	☐	☐	☐
I work with the multidisciplinary team to determine whether my students should take general grade level assessments or alternate assessments.	☐	☐	☐	☐
Testing accommodations for my students provide them with access to tests without altering the content, constructs, or results of my tests or giving them an advantage over their classmates.	☐	☐	☐	☐
I consider providing my students with a range of presentation mode testing accommodations.	☐	☐	☐	☐
I consider providing my students with a range of response mode testing accommodations.	☐	☐	☐	☐
I consider providing my students with a range of timing, scheduling, and setting testing accommodations.	☐	☐	☐	☐
I consider providing my students with a range of linguistically based testing accommodations.	☐	☐	☐	☐
I consider using a range of grading alternatives cautiously and occasionally to motivate my students and reinforce their efforts to succeed on tests.	☐	☐	☐	☐
Decisions regarding the use of specific testing accommodations for my students are individually determined based on their unique characteristics and learning strengths and challenges.	☐	☐	☐	☐

(Continued)

Figure 2.6 (Continued)

Keys to Best Practice	Often	Sometimes	Rarely	Never
Testing accommodations for my students match the effective teaching accommodations they regularly use in daily classroom instruction.	☐	☐	☐	☐
Decisions regarding testing accommodations for my students comply with statewide and districtwide policies.	☐	☐	☐	☐
Testing accommodations for my students during high-stakes and districtwide assessments and teacher-made tests are differentiated, and these distinctions are made explicit via their IEPs and 504 accommodation plans.	☐	☐	☐	☐
Efforts are made to match my students' testing accommodations for teacher-made tests with those allowed for high-stakes tests.	☐	☐	☐	☐
The perspectives of my students are considered in determining their testing accommodations.	☐	☐	☐	☐
Testing accommodations selected for my students with disabilities boost their performance and have a limited impact on the performance of their classmates.	☐	☐	☐	☐
The perspectives of teachers are considered in determining testing accommodations for my students.	☐	☐	☐	☐
The implementation of my students' testing accommodations is fostered via their IEPs and 504 accommodation plans.	☐	☐	☐	☐
Evaluation data are collected on my students' use of testing accommodations.	☐	☐	☐	☐
Evaluation data are used to determine whether my students' testing accommodations should be continued, revised, discontinued, or gradually faded out.	☐	☐	☐	☐

- How would you rate your ability to determine and implement valid and appropriate testing accommodations for your students?
- What aspects are your strengths?
- In what areas do you need to improve?
- What steps can you take to improve your ability to determine and implement valid and appropriate testing accommodations for your students?

3

Using Technology-Based Testing

Ms. Randolph, a general educator, and Mr. Smith, a special education teacher, had worked as a cooperative teaching team for several years. Knowing that their students benefited from using technology, they had integrated a wide range of instructional technologies into their classroom to differentiate their instruction. They noticed that their students were particularly excited about using technology and that it helped motivate them to learn and complete their assignments.

However, Ms. Randolph and Mr. Smith were disappointed that many of their students still performed poorly on tests and quizzes. They discussed the possible reasons for the discrepancy between their students' classroom and testing performances and decided that they needed to use technology to make their testing conditions more like their classroom instructional techniques. The teachers shared their goals with Ms. Rodriguez, the school's instructional technology (IT) specialist, who was eager to work with them.

The three teachers began researching the ways to use technology-based testing by reviewing relevant Web sites and resources. Ms. Rodriguez obtained additional information by posting an inquiry on a Listserv used by professionals interested in educational technology. Several local educators who responded invited the teachers to visit their classrooms. On these visits, they learned how others were using technology to create and administer tests to students.

As the teachers learned more about using technology-based testing, they realized there were many different ways to use it, so they developed a plan to implement it in steps. They began by using technology to improve the readability and the format of their tests so that the tests were easier for students to complete (see Chapter 1). Soon their students started taking online quizzes. As students became more familiar with the technology-based testing format, the teachers gradually converted their tests to PDF files that students could complete via the computer. For their students with reading difficulties, the teachers used text-to-speech and optical character recognition systems to help these students read test directions and items.

Although they noted an improvement in their students' test grades, the teachers also had some concerns. Some of their students did not feel comfortable taking tests via technology, and the teachers were concerned that students might access online resources while taking tests. After meeting with Ms. Rodriguez to discuss these issues, they decided to give students opportunities to take practice tests using technology and to establish rules and procedures to prevent online cheating. As everyone became more comfortable using technology-based testing, the teachers used other technologies to add new features.

- Does your school use technology-based testing?
- How does it work?
- How do your students feel about taking tests via technology?
- What are the advantages and challenges of using technology-based testing?

Educators like Ms. Randolph and Mr. Smith are realizing that technology offers innovative ways to help their students take tests (Thompson, Quenemoen, & Thurlow, 2006). Technology-based testing has many advantages that can benefit you, your students, and their families. Technology can help you incorporate the principles of universal design for learning (UDL) and visual design so that your testing materials are laid out appropriately and accessible to and useable by students who have a wide range of ability levels (see Chapter 1; Ketterlin-Geller et al., 2007). Technology allows you to deliver a range of testing accommodations that are tailored to the unique strengths and challenges of your students and to decrease the time spent giving, grading, and analyzing student performance on tests.

For your students, taking tests via technology can be a more motivating and successful experience as they can select various test administration options and receive prompt feedback on their performance. In particular, technology-based testing can increase the participation of students with disabilities in standardized and teacher-made testing programs (Ketterlin-Geller et al., 2007). Technology-based testing has advantages for families as it has the potential to enhance the test performance of their children and the speed at which test results are shared with them.

In light of the potential advantages of technology-based testing, this chapter offers you a variety of best practices for using technology-based testing (we will learn about how you can use technology to implement a variety of classroom assessments in Chapter 5). These practices can be combined with those presented in Chapters 1 and 2 to enhance the testing experience for your students by providing alternate and novel ways to

- enhance student motivation and feedback,
- present test directions and items to students, and
- facilitate students' responses to test items.

Specifically, this chapter addresses the following questions:

- How can technology-based testing be used to enhance student motivation and feedback and minimize student errors?
- How can technology-based testing be used to present test directions and items to students?
- How can technology-based testing be used to help students respond to objective test questions?
- How can technology-based testing be used to help students respond to essay test questions?
- What concerns need to be considered and addressed when using technology-based testing?

While this chapter offers a range of suggestions, resources, and technologies, it is recommended that you proceed gradually and start your efforts to use technology-based testing with a limited number of features. As you and your students and their families become comfortable with using technology-based testing, additional features can be gradually introduced. Furthermore, since testing conditions should parallel instructional conditions, the technology used by your students during testing should be introduced to them and used regularly in daily classroom instruction.

Appendix A offers a listing of Web sites related to the resources mentioned in this chapter. Prior to using these technology resources, you should carefully evaluate them in terms of their ease of use, design, contents, accessibility, options, navigability, and appropriateness for use by you and your students (Boone & Higgins, 2007). Figure 3.1 offers guidelines you can use to evaluate technology-based testing resources.

Figure 3.1 Evaluating Technology-Based Testing Resources

Technology-Based Testing Features	Excellent	Good	Fair	Needs Improvement
Goals and purposes are stated and appropriate	☐	☐	☐	☐
Students will find the resource welcoming and user friendly	☐	☐	☐	☐
Directions are clear, understandable, easy to follow, and can be repeated	☐	☐	☐	☐
Directions can be presented in multiple formats (text, audio, video)	☐	☐	☐	☐
Students can use the resource independently	☐	☐	☐	☐
Relevant features are easily identified and clearly labeled	☐	☐	☐	☐
Tutorials to teach students how to use the resource and features are offered	☐	☐	☐	☐
Opportunities for students to practice are provided	☐	☐	☐	☐
Help and search features are available	☐	☐	☐	☐
Links are clearly identified and labeled	☐	☐	☐	☐
Links are appropriate, helpful, and active	☐	☐	☐	☐
Program loads quickly and consistently	☐	☐	☐	☐
Content is current, accurate, relevant, and credible	☐	☐	☐	☐
Content and visual images are presented in multiple formats and in an organized, consistent, uncluttered, sequential, and logical manner	☐	☐	☐	☐
Content is free of errors and bias and revised regularly	☐	☐	☐	☐
Content is developmentally and age appropriate	☐	☐	☐	☐
The difficulty levels of the content can be adjusted	☐	☐	☐	☐
Content can be branched based on prior responses of students	☐	☐	☐	☐
Numerous opportunities to respond to similar content and items are available	☐	☐	☐	☐
Content, directions, and items can be revised, deleted, and added	☐	☐	☐	☐

(Continued)

Figure 3.1 (Continued)

Technology-Based Testing Features	Excellent	Good	Fair	Needs Improvement
Language is age-appropriate and free of biases	☐	☐	☐	☐
Text is readable at the appropriate grade level	☐	☐	☐	☐
Reading levels can be adjusted	☐	☐	☐	☐
Digital speech of text and audio descriptions of visual images are available	☐	☐	☐	☐
Options to facilitate use by students with disabilities are available, intuitive, and easy to use	☐	☐	☐	☐
Response formats are varied, obvious, and easy for students	☐	☐	☐	☐
Use of alternate input devices is facilitated	☐	☐	☐	☐
Limited keyboarding skills are required	☐	☐	☐	☐
Options to facilitate use by English language learners are available, intuitive, and easy to use	☐	☐	☐	☐
Error minimization techniques are included	☐	☐	☐	☐
Links are available to support other technologies designed for students with special needs	☐	☐	☐	☐
Text size, font, color, style variants, spacing, and backgrounds can be adjusted	☐	☐	☐	☐
Size, color, and backgrounds of visual images can be adjusted	☐	☐	☐	☐
Speed, amount, time, and sequence of the presentation of and response to content and items can be adjusted by students and teachers	☐	☐	☐	☐
Ways to highlight important words and content (e.g., color cuing, boldface, italics) are provided	☐	☐	☐	☐
Animation and sound can be enabled or disabled	☐	☐	☐	☐
Auditory and visual cues and prompts can be provided	☐	☐	☐	☐
Content and directions can be presented in alternate formats and revised by teachers	☐	☐	☐	☐
Content and items can be presented in a game format with specialized effects (sound, animation, video, etc.)	☐	☐	☐	☐

Technology-Based Testing Features	Excellent	Good	Fair	Needs Improvement
Student attention and motivation are maintained	☐	☐	☐	☐
Screen design is clear, nondistracting uncluttered, appropriate, intuitive, and consistent	☐	☐	☐	☐
Menus and navigational features are clearly presented in multiple formats (text, icons, audio) and intuitive	☐	☐	☐	☐
Opportunities to review individual and cumulative responses are provided	☐	☐	☐	☐
Items and responses can be easily retrieved and revised	☐	☐	☐	☐
Navigation back and forth is simple and logical	☐	☐	☐	☐
Informative and corrective feedback are provided	☐	☐	☐	☐
Feedback is immediate, positive, and consistent	☐	☐	☐	☐
Feedback can be individualized and personalized	☐	☐	☐	☐
Student responses are recorded automatically, promptly, and over time	☐	☐	☐	☐
Student responses are easily accessed	☐	☐	☐	☐
Quick and accurate results are provided in an understandable format	☐	☐	☐	☐
Hardware and software requirements are listed	☐	☐	☐	☐
Prerequisite skills needed for use are presented	☐	☐	☐	☐
Developer is identified and has credibility	☐	☐	☐	☐
Documentation and research to support use and effectiveness are provided	☐	☐	☐	☐
Contact information is provided	☐	☐	☐	☐
Technical assistance is readily available and helpful	☐	☐	☐	☐
Cost is reasonable	☐	☐	☐	☐

Additional Comments:

Sources: Boone & Higgins, 2007; Salend, 2008.

When selecting technology-based testing techniques, you must consider whether the technology provides your students with access to tests without altering the test's integrity. For example, although using audio technology to read test items would not be appropriate when taking a reading test, as it changes the nature of the test to one assessing listening comprehension, it might be appropriate for use when taking tests that are designed to assess other skills such as mathematics, science, or social studies. Therefore, before using the technology-based testing features presented in this chapter, you need to consider whether they change the content and results of your tests.

HOW CAN TECHNOLOGY-BASED TESTING BE USED TO ENHANCE STUDENT MOTIVATION AND FEEDBACK AND MINIMIZE STUDENT ERRORS?

Keys to Best Practice: Use technology to create and administer tests that enhance student motivation (Salend, 2009; Thompson et al., 2006).

Technology-based testing can help you enhance your students' motivation by allowing you to (a) tailor the administration of your tests to their skill levels, (b) accommodate their scheduling preferences, (c) deliver reinforcement and encouragement to students, (d) use academic game formats, (e) provide real-time feedback, and (f) embed error minimization techniques into tests. These technologies are presented below.

Keys to Best Practice: Use technology to tailor the administration of tests to the skill levels of your students so that the difficulty of each question depends on how they performed on the prior question(s) (Bouck, 2006; Geller, 2005).

Tailoring the Administration of Tests to Students' Skill Levels

You can motivate your students to complete tests by using technology-based testing to tailor the administration of tests to their skill levels (Bouck, 2006). For example, an exam can be presented via computers so that the difficulty of each succeeding question depends on how students performed on the prior question(s). If students answer a question correctly, the computer branches to a more difficult item. If students answer a question incorrectly, the computer presents an easier item to them. Student performance on these exams can then be based on their correct responses and the level of difficulty.

Keys to Best Practice: Use technology to accommodate the individual testing schedule preferences of students and teachers (Beddow, Kettler, & Elliott, 2008; Geller, 2005).

Accommodating Scheduling Preferences

The flexibility associated with technology-based testing can motivate your students by accommodating their individualized scheduling preferences by allowing for extended time, breaks, multiple testing sessions, time of day and location considerations, and variations in the pace and sequence in which tests are administered. For example, your students can take tests over several days, and their responses can be cumulative and revised up to the point that they submit it. Your students also can take breaks and be directed to the part of the test they were working on before the break.

Via technology, students with motor difficulties can take self-paced tests that allow you and them to make adjustments based on the time they need to complete the whole test or specific items. Technology also can provide students with an on-screen clock and indicator that informs students of the time and the amount of time left to complete the test (Beddow et al., 2008).

Keys to Best Practice: Use technology to motivate students by providing them with reinforcement and encouragement related to their responses and their testing behaviors (Bennett, Zentall, French, & Giorgetti-Borucki, 2006).

Delivering Reinforcement and Encouragement

Technology-based testing can foster student motivation by providing your students with reinforcement and encouragement related to correct responses and appropriate testing behaviors. Thus, after answering a predetermined question or questions, computers can deliver a reinforcing visual or auditory event to students to acknowledge their performance or behavior. For example, via technology-based testing, your students can periodically receive reinforcement and encouragement (e.g., *Congratulations, you are finished with the multiple-choice questions*) and prompts to remind them to stay focused and motivated and to engage in self-reinforcement (e.g., *Keep working hard. Give yourself a high-five*). Your students also can be provided choices regarding the frequency they receive reinforcement and encouragement when they take technology-based tests (Bennett et al., 2006).

Keys to Best Practice: Use technology to present tests and quizzes in academic game formats (Barlow & Wetherill, 2005; Bouck, 2006; Mounce, 2008; Shaffer, 2007).

Using Academic Game Formats

Student motivation and on-task behavior can be promoted by presenting tests and quizzes using game software programs and Internet-based academic games. In particular, your students may be motivated by tests and quizzes that are presented via video, interactive boards, PowerPoint, or collaborative game formats (Barlow & Wetherill, 2005; Mounce, 2008). Additional information and resources for creating technology-based tests and quizzes using game formats are presented in Chapter 5 and Appendix A and Appendix B.

Keys to Best Practice: Use technology to provide students with real-time feedback related to their test performance (Bennett et al. 2006; Salend, 2009; Thompson et al., 2006).

Providing Real-Time Feedback

Technology-based tests can support student motivation and learning by providing students with real-time feedback related to test performance and by allowing students to take tests and quizzes multiple times. During initial testing, incorrect responses can result in immediate feedback that provides students with information about the correct answers, guides students in understanding why their answers are incorrect, and offers supplemental activities to help students learn the material. After reviewing this information and performing these alternate learning activities, students can take another version of the test or quiz to improve their score and to demonstrate mastery of the material.

Keys to Best Practice: Use technology-based testing to help your students identify correct and incorrect answers, the types of errors made, and the topics and concepts that they need to review (Bouck, 2006; Salend, 2009).

After taking tests or quizzes, students can receive immediate feedback about their performance. In addition to obtaining their score, technology-based testing can help you and your students identify correct and incorrect answers, the types of errors made, and the topics and concepts that they need to review. You and your students can then examine these data to assess why specific answers were incorrect and what actions can be taken to help them learn the content being assessed.

Keys to Best Practice: Use technology to embed error minimization techniques into tests to motivate your students by limiting their test-taking errors (Dolan, Hall, Banerjee, Chun, & Strangman, 2005; Stock, Davies, & Wehmeyer, 2004).

Embedding Error Minimization Techniques

Technology-based tests that contain embedded error minimization techniques can help motivate students by limiting their test-taking errors. Via technology, your tests can include error minimization techniques such as

- presenting only one test item on the screen at a time;
- making sure that your students respond to a test item before they are allowed to move to the next item;
- pairing entered responses to items with visuals, animation, videos and pictorials, and sounds such as an automated visual animation and oral recording stating the answer option selected (e.g., A, B, C, or D, or true-false);
- linking icons and text to guide students throughout the test (*Go to the next section*);

- saving students' answers automatically; and
- allowing students to check their responses by viewing the items they have completed, or accessing or reviewing any test items or sections at any time.

HOW CAN TECHNOLOGY-BASED TESTING BE USED TO PRESENT TEST DIRECTIONS AND ITEMS TO STUDENTS?

Keys to Best Practice: Use a range of technologies that allows your students to make choices about the ways test items and directions are presented to them (Beddow et al., 2008; Hansen & Mislevy, 2006; Thompson et al., 2006).

Technology has the potential to deliver a range of presentation mode testing accommodations. Technologies are available that provide you and your students with choices about the ways in which test directions and items are presented to students. Using these technologies, you and your students can select options that allow your students to

- hear test directions and items multiple times;
- highlight text and make drawings and notes to guide them in taking tests and responding to questions;
- access links to electronic resources such as dictionaries, glossaries and thesauri, strategy reminders, and pop-up definitions and translations;
- adjust text, images, and backgrounds in terms of print sizes, colors, fonts, spacing, and layout;
- eliminate backgrounds, sounds, animations, and images; and
- control the pace of the test administration, the sequence in which items are presented, and the number of items that appear on the screen at a time (Beddow et al., 2008).

Technologies to tailor the presentation of test directions and items can be especially helpful for your students with reading difficulties, students with sensory disabilities, and students who are English language learners.

Students With Reading Difficulties

Your students, particularly those with visual and reading disabilities, can benefit from a range of technologies that presents test directions and items orally. These technologies include screen or text readers, scanners, and optical character reading systems (OCRs), which allow text and visuals to be presented with audio. They also include low-tech devices that can facilitate reading.

Keys to Best Practice: Consider presenting tests to your students using a range of screen- or text-reading programs (Hasselbring & Bausch, 2006; Hopkins, 2006).

Screen and Text Readers

Screen and text readers allow your students to hear test directions and items read aloud to them including audio descriptions of visual images (Hasselbring & Bausch, 2006). These programs, which can read text aloud in different voices and languages, provide your students with ways to search for or highlight words, sentences, and paragraphs that can be read aloud to them. Many of these programs also can be customized to the individual preferences of your students by allowing them to

- control the speed, pitch, and volume of the speech;
- create pronunciation dictionaries; and
- have text digitally highlighted on the computer screen as it is read aloud to students.

Screen-reading programs can be programmed to provide students with visual impairments with verbal descriptions of images, pictorials, and graphics. For example, WebAnywhere (webanywhere.cs.washington.edu) is a free online self-voicing screen reader that can be used with all types of computers to convert online text, graphics, and photographs to an audio file that is orally presented to students. A listing of text- and screen-reading programs is presented in Appendix A.

Screen- and text-reading programs also are available on computers that have newer operating systems. For instance, the "Save as DAISY XML" feature (www.daisy.org/projects/save-as-daisy-microsoft) can convert text-based Word documents, such as your tests and other print materials, into Digital Accessible Information SYstem (DAISY) files, accessible formats that can be orally presented to your students with visual impairments and students with reading difficulties. Additional information about DAISY can be obtained at the DAISY Consortium's Web site, www.daisy.org.

Keys to Best Practice: Consider presenting tests to your students using text scanners and OCRs (Higgins & Raskind, 2005; Salend, 2008; Thompson, Bakken, Fulk, & Peterson-Karlan, 2005).

Text Scanners and OCRs

As Ms. Randolph and Mr. Smith did, you can present your tests to your students by using text scanners and OCRs with speech-reading capabilities.

Using these technologies, you would use the following procedure:

1. Prepare valid and accessible tests following the guidelines presented in Chapter 1.

2. Scan your tests and store them in a computer.

3. Use OCRs to read tests aloud to your students.

Your students also can use small and portable OCRs to take their printed tests (see Appendix A). These technologies contain functions that allow your students to scan sentences and words in a test's directions and items and control whether they want the scanned text to be read, defined, spelled, or displayed in various character sizes. Many of these devices can present dictionary and thesaurus entries and can translate text into a variety of languages, which make them particularly helpful for your students who are English language learners.

When considering using scanners and OCRs, it is important for you to carefully examine the ability of the scanner to scan accurately. Remember that portable OCR systems are most useful for reading words or sentences rather than long paragraphs or pages.

Keys to Best Practice: Consider presenting tests to your students using a range of low-tech devices (Parette, Wojcik, Peterson-Karlan, & Hourcade, 2005; Salend, 2008; Thompson et al., 2005).

Low-Tech Devices

Low-tech devices, which are usually inexpensive, nonelectric, readily available, and homemade, can be used to facilitate the presentation of tests to students with reading difficulties. Line guides or masks, such as reading rulers or index cards, can assist students who have difficulty tracking and maintaining their place on a line. Some of your students also may benefit from placing colored acetate overlays on their tests to help them adjust the contrast in the text. For example, the Visual Tracking Magnifier (www.coil.co.uk) is a small handheld device that assists students in reading and maintaining their place by magnifying a line of text and providing transparent overlays that modify the background colors of pages (Thompson et al., 2005).

Keys to Best Practice: Consider presenting tests to your students with visual impairments using a range of technologies (Brody, 2006; Curry, 2003; Hopkins, 2006; Neal & Ehlert, 2006).

Students With Sensory Disabilities

Technology can be used to help your students with sensory disabilities access test directions and items. In addition to some of the technologies that read online text and graphics to students, your students with visual impairments may benefit from using the following technology:

- Screen magnification and contrast, font enlargement programs as well as technologies that allow them to zoom in on item features (see Appendix A)
- External magnification devices that are placed over the monitors to allow them to adjust technology-generated text and graphics to an appropriate size, font, color, and contrast
- Programs that provide audio descriptions of visual images
- Flicker-free monitors that have a higher resolution and contrast

You also can use technology to provide these students with photo-enlarged examinations and answer sheets, and Braille or large-print versions of tests (Hopkins, 2006). For example, Visiprint (www.visiprintsoftware.com) offers a range of software programs that can help you prepare large print documents that can be tailored to the different needs and preferences of your students with visual impairments.

Keys to Best Practice: Consider presenting tests to your deaf and hard of hearing students using a range of technologies (Hopkins, 2006; Jones, 2008; Salend, 2008).

Your deaf and hard of hearing students may benefit from a range of assistive listening technologies that can help them access orally presented tests (see Appendix A). Since your classroom probably has a variety of background noises that can interfere with test performance, sound-field amplification devices that use FM and wireless technology can be employed to increase the ability of your students to hear the test administrator's voice and help them focus their attention on verbal information (Jones, 2008). While these systems are designed for use by your hard of hearing students, they also can be useful for your students with attention difficulties.

There are two types of sound-field amplification systems: sound-field and personal FM (Dell, Newton, & Petroff, 2008; Hopkins, 2006). Both systems involve your wearing a small and lightweight, wireless microphone and transmitter. In the sound-field system, your voice is amplified for all of your students via a central receiver and loudspeaker located in your classroom. In the personal FM system, individual students wear headphones with a receiver that allows them to hear your voice more clearly. When using these systems, you need to remember to turn them off when you are speaking directly or confidentially to specific students or to other professionals. While both systems are effective, sound-field systems tend to be cheaper, and their use does not embarrass individual students; they do not feel different since your voice is amplified for all students.

Your deaf and hard of hearing students may use closed-captioning, sign, or pictorially based test presentation formats (Salend, 2008). These students also can access computer presented information via text-to-sign language converters whereby the text and graphics appear on the monitor accompanied by a video of a signer who signs the text. For students who have some hearing, a digitized voice can read the test items and directions as the signer signs it.

Keys to Best Practice: Consider presenting tests to your students who are English language learners using a range of technologies (Hansen & Mislevy, 2006; Salend, 2008; Wang, 2005).

English Language Learners

Technology-based testing can be used to present tests to your students who are English language learners. Various technologies can be used to allow your students who are English language learners to take tests administered in their preferred language, and to access bilingual dictionaries, glossaries, and thesauri and pop-up translations. They can use handheld talking translators or translation software programs that convert text from one language into another. For example, the *Quicktionary* (www.easytranslators.com/factfile/wizcom.htm) is a pen-like device that scans text in one language and translates it into another language. When using these programs, it is important for you and your students to understand that they may at times provide inaccurate translations and may not cover the range of dialects associated with specific languages. Therefore, you need to prescreen your tests using these devices to make sure their use is appropriate.

HOW CAN TECHNOLOGY-BASED TESTING BE USED TO HELP STUDENTS RESPOND TO OBJECTIVE TEST QUESTIONS?

In addition to using technology to access test directions and items, many students may need to use a range of technologies to respond to objective test questions. These technologies are described below.

Keys to Best Practice: Consider providing alternate methods to access and use technology for your students with motor difficulties (Dell et al., 2008; Hopkins, 2006; Neal & Ehlert, 2006; Wissick, 2005).

Students With Motor Difficulties

Some of your students, especially those with motor difficulties, may have problems using technology in traditional ways (Hopkins, 2006). These students may need to use alternative methods to access technology such as adapted switches, scanning systems, joysticks, headbands, and sip and puff systems (Dell et al., 2008). They also may benefit from using larger, ergonomic, and alternative keyboards that can be placed at different angles and have different letter, key, and spacing arrangements (see Appendix A). Some of your students may need to use keyboards that have auditory keys that offer oral feedback when they are accessed, key guards, stickers to signify keys, and key locks (Wissick, 2005). They may find the following built-in accessibility features useful:

- *StickyKeys*, which can be used so that one key press causes the technology to take actions that are associated with multiple keys being pressed simultaneously
- *MouseKeys*, which allow students to direct the mouse pointer with one finger, a mouthstick, or a headpointer by using the numeric keypad to move the mouse pointer
- *ToggleKeys*, which use a beeping sound to alert students when certain features are activated such as the lock keys NUM LOCK, CAPS LOCK, or SCROLL LOCK
- *FilterKeys*, which contain a variety of features related to adjusting the keyboard response time and dealing with inadvertent pressing of keys
- *RepeatKeys*, which provide students with control over whether repeated key strokes are converted into computer actions and allow students to adjust the repeat start time and rate
- *BounceKeys*, which allow students who bounce when activating or releasing a key to access only one action or keyboard character

Your students with tremors or uncontrolled hand or finger movements may need to use an adapted mouse that can adjust for extraneous movements. Some of your students may find it helpful to use other built-in accessibility features such as on-screen keyboarding, touch screens, visual and auditory warnings, and high-lighted mouse visibility and movement (Dell et al., 2008; Neal & Ehlert, 2006). For example, PointSmart (www.infogrip.com/product_view.asp?RecordNumber=988) allows you and your students to adjust the speed of the cursor and the mouse.

Keys to Best Practice: Consider whether your students' responses to test items can be facilitated by use of voice-recognition and voice-activated systems (Fitzgerald, 2008; Pogue, 2008; Silver-Pacuilla & Fleischman, 2006).

Voice-Recognition and Voice-Activated Systems

Student responses to test items may be facilitated by using voice-recognition and voice-activated systems (see Appendix A; Fitzgerald, 2008; Silver-Pacuilla & Fleischman, 2006). These systems, which are particularly useful for your students who have difficulty typing, convert students' spoken words into text or into actions that activate technology and computerized menus. For instance, students can access menus or Web site links by stating an action or a name. Using these programs, your students complete tests by dictating their answers into the computer and then editing and spell checking their responses via use of word processing. While these systems continue to have improved accuracy rates and can recognize the different accents of students from different regions in the United States (e.g., Great Lakes, southern United States) and students from other parts of the world (e.g., Australia, Britain, Southeast Asia, India, Mexico, Spain, Pogue, 2008), it is important to remember some difficulties recognizing your students' speech may occur. In addition, your students may need assistance in learning how to use these programs effectively and training the programs to recognize and respond to their voices.

Keys to Best Practice: Consider using a range of technologies to help your students who have difficulty responding orally or in writing take tests (Bouck & Bouck, 2008; Dell et al., 2008; Hopkins, 2006; Parette et al., 2005).

Other Technologies

Augmentative communication systems (see Appendix A), Braille writers, pointers, electronic dictionaries and thesauri, and digital recorders can help your students who find responding orally or in writing a challenge (Dell et al., 2008; Parette et al., 2005). Talking calculators, software programs, and personal digital assistants (PDAs) can be helpful for students who have the conceptual understanding to complete items but lack the memory skills to remember math computations, facts, or word definitions (Bouck & Bouck, 2008).

HOW CAN TECHNOLOGY-BASED TESTING BE USED TO HELP STUDENTS RESPOND TO ESSAY TEST QUESTIONS?

Keys to Best Practice: Consider using a variety of technologies to aid your students in composing written responses to essay questions (Cullen, Richards, & Frank, 2008; MacArthur, 2009).

In addition to the alternate ways to respond to objective test questions we just discussed, a variety of technologies can guide your students through the writing process, which can aid them in composing written responses to essay questions (MacArthur, 2009). These technologies and resources, which are discussed below, should be selected based on your students' strengths and challenges (Cullen et al., 2008).

Keys to Best Practice: Consider allowing your students to use appropriate word processing programs to compose their essays (Lindstrom, 2007; MacArthur, 2009; Silver-Pacuilla & Fleischman, 2005).

Word Processing

Word processing can make it easier to compose and revise written responses and minimize handwriting problems so your students can produce complete, organized, and legible essays (MacArthur, 2009). In choosing an appropriate word processing program for your students to use when composing their essays, consider whether the programs

- include directions and menus that are easy to read and follow;
- prompt students using pictures and cues;
- use simple keystrokes;
- provide access to electronic dictionaries, thesauri, and glossaries that can guide them in making varied word choices;
- offer prompting and verification to help students save files and access features; and
- have safeguards to prevent the loss of files (Hetzroni & Shrieber, 2004).

Your students with reading and visual disabilities may benefit from using talking and talk-type word processors (Parette et al., 2005, see Appendix A). Talking word processors that "read" the text on the computer screen can assist these students in detecting written language errors by providing feedback on spelling as they type words and allowing them to listen to their text being read. These applications can be combined with *text windowing*, the simultaneous visual highlighting of text as it is read to help your students focus on, monitor, and proofread their essays.

Talk-type or voice-activated word-processing programs based on computerized speech recognition may be especially appropriate for your students who struggle with written communication but have strong verbal communication skills (Silver-Pacuilla & Fleischman, 2005). These programs allow your students to view their dictated statements as text on a monitor and then revise them by stating the word processing actions to be taken. In using these systems, your students should be taught how to correct errors as well as be reminded to speak clearly, to avoid making extraneous sounds, and to state punctuation marks (MacArthur, 2009).

Some of your students with writing and motor difficulties may benefit from use of word processing programs with abbreviation expanders (Lindstrom, 2007). These word processing programs convert abbreviations for commonly used words, phrases, and sentences into full text.

Keys to Best Practice: Consider allowing your students to use spell checkers to compose their essays (MacArthur, 2009; Moats, 2006).

Spell Checkers

Word processing programs offer a range of different types of spell checkers to help your students identify and correct spelling errors in their test responses. Some of your students who struggle with reading may benefit from using spell checkers that read word choices to them, while other students may prefer a system that provides a definition of each word presented as an alternative. Spell checkers that identify homonyms and prompt students to check them and programs that orally present words in the correct list or present word choices in short lists may assist many students (MacArthur, 2009).

Keys to Best Practice: Consider allowing your students to use word cueing and prediction programs to compose their essays (Hasselbring & Bausch, 2006; MacArthur, 2009; Wissick, 2005).

Word Cueing and Prediction

Your students' ability to write responses to essay test questions can be facilitated by their use of word cueing and prediction programs (see Appendix A). These types of programs, which offer students choices of words and phrases as they compose text, are particularly helpful for students who have difficulty recalling words and using a variety of words (Hasselbring & Bausch, 2006; Wissick, 2005). When using these types of programs, a changing list of predicted words and phrases appears on the screen as your students type their essays. Your students can then decide whether or not to select the predicted or cued word(s) and insert them into the sentences that make up their essays. The size and the words and phrases in the banks that are integral parts of these programs can be customized for your students based on their strengths and challenges and the topics and concepts being tested (MacArthur, 2009). Thus, when students are taking a social studies test, the word bank can be tailored to include words from the social studies content being assessed.

Word cueing and prediction programs differ in the ways in which they prompt students. Word choices provided in word cueing programs are based on the first letters typed by students. Word prediction programs offer word and phrase options based on context, word frequency (i.e., how frequently the word is used in English), word recency (i.e., how recently the word has been used by the writer), grammatical correctness, and commonly associated words and phrases.

Keys to Best Practice: Consider allowing your students to use electronic dictionaries, glossaries, and thesauri to compose their essays (Zorfass, Fideler, Clay, & Brann, 2007).

Electronic Dictionaries, Glossaries, and Thesauri

While working on their essays, your students may benefit from using electronic dictionaries and thesauri (see Appendix A), which can help them understand and define words or identify synonyms and other words to use in writing their responses (Zorfass et al., 2007). Since many of these programs use multimedia such as animations, 3-D visuals, colorful graphics, and audio pronunciations to help students understand and learn word meanings and determine appropriate alternative words and phrases, these programs are particularly helpful for your students who are English language learners. However, when using these programs, you should consider whether they serve to inadvertently overstimulate your students and hinder their test performance.

Keys to Best Practice: Consider allowing your students to use text organization, word usage, and grammar and punctuation assistance resources to compose their essays (MacArthur, 2009; Parette et al., 2005; Salend, 2008).

Text Organization, Word Usage, and Grammar and Punctuation Assistance Resources

Your students' abilities to plan and compose their essays can be facilitated by using visual and auditory prompts, outlining, semantic mapping, and graphics-based writing programs and multimedia (MacArthur, 2009; Parette et al., 2005). Graphics-based writing software programs, which offer storyboarding and framing, pictures, video, sound, animation, and voice recording, can motivate your students and assist them in planning, organizing, and composing text related to essay questions. Software programs that offer your students access to outlines and semantic maps can help them plan, organize, and develop their essay responses (see Appendix A).

Word usage and grammar checkers as well as punctuation assistance programs can help your students identify inappropriate word choices and grammatical and punctuation errors in their responses to essay questions and present alternatives to revise them (see Appendix A; Salend, 2008). Your students can use these programs to view identified errors and then examine the alternatives and select the option they believe best corrects the error. Many of these programs can guide your students in selecting an appropriate alternative by offering prompts, as well as reviews and explanations of the different selections and their corresponding word meanings and grammatical applications. Features such as automatic correction, available in many word processing programs (e.g., AutoCorrect in Microsoft Word), can be employed by your students to guide them in producing grammatically correct essay responses. For instance, these programs can be set to automatically capitalize proper nouns and the first words of sentences.

Keys to Best Practice: Consider allowing your students to use essay grading and feedback resources to compose their essays (MacArthur, 2009; Sedensky, 2005).

Essay Grading and Feedback Resources

Essay grading and feedback resources can help your students improve the quality of their responses to essay questions (see Appendix A). Using these programs, your students

- submit their essays electronically;
- receive immediate detailed feedback concerning their essays' content, style, word choices, organization, mechanics, and conventions; and
- use the feedback to revise their essay responses (MacArthur, 2009).

WHAT CONCERNS NEED TO BE CONSIDERED AND ADDRESSED WHEN USING TECHNOLOGY-BASED TESTING?

Technology-based testing holds great promise for facilitating the testing process for teachers, students, and families. However, as Ms. Randolph and Mr. Smith found, it is important for you to be aware of and address concerns associated with its use including bridging the *digital divide*, preventing high-tech cheating, limiting distracting features, and fostering student and teacher preparation.

Keys to Best Practice: Be aware of and address the *digital divide* (Kalyanpur & Kirmani, 2005; Prensky, 2008).

Bridging the Digital Divide

While technology has become an important tool to support and assess student learning, the *digital divide* is a concern, which can exacerbate some of the inequities that already exist in classrooms, schools, and society (Kalyanpur & Kirmani, 2005; Prensky, 2008). The digital divide means that many of your students with disabilities, your students from culturally and linguistically diverse backgrounds, your students living in poverty, and your female students may encounter barriers that affect their access to and use of technology. Thus, your students who have limited experience with technology or who use inefficient or dated hardware and software are placed at a significant disadvantage when taking technology-based tests. For example, inexperience with taking tests using technology can affect the testing experience for students, making it longer and more tiring for students.

Keys to Best Practice: Provide your students with numerous opportunities to use technology in daily classroom instructional activities (MacArthur, 2009; Salend, 2008).

Fostering Student Preparation

While bridging the digital divide is a challenge that requires multifaceted solutions, you can work toward providing all of your students with the preparation they need to use a wide range of technologies (Salend, 2008). Like Ms. Randolph and Mr. Smith, you can offer numerous opportunities to use technology in your daily classroom instructional activities. We will learn more about other ways you can use technology to implement classroom assessments in Chapter 5.

Keys to Best Practice: Explicitly teach your students the skills they need to use specific technologies and to take technology-based tests (Beddow et al., 2008; Bouck, 2006; Edyburn, 2003; Salend, 2009).

Since taking tests via technology requires some unique test-taking skills and strategies, it is important for you to explicitly teach your students the skills needed to use specific technologies (Salend, 2009). For example, your students may need to develop their keyboarding skills and learn how to highlight and return to test questions that they need to review as well as how to revise or change answers.

You can use test and quiz creation programs to provide your students with opportunities to take practice tests using the technology-based testing format they will use on their actual tests (Beddow et al., 2008). Technology-based practice tests also can be designed to develop both your students' content mastery and their technology-based test-taking skills and strategies (see Appendix A). Thus, if students answer a practice question correctly, a screen can appear

- explaining why the answer is correct,
- providing additional information about the test content,
- pointing out why the other answers are incorrect (in the case of multiple-choice items), and
- presenting effective test-taking skills and strategies that can be used to answer the question.

Additionally, if your students answer a practice question incorrectly, they can be provided with an opportunity to access additional information and resources about the facts, concepts, and topics being assessed as well as effective test-taking skills and strategies that can be used to answer the question. For instance, you can use LS Test Builder (www.learningstation.com/solutions/test_builder.html) to provide your students with study guides based on their performance on practice tests that are linked to your curriculum and your state's mandated tests. Your students can visit Web sites that provide information about and practice opportunities for technology-based tests (see Appendix A; Bouck, 2006). We will discuss other effective study and test-taking skills and strategies your students can learn to enhance their testing performance in Chapter 4.

Keys to Best Practice: Be aware of high-tech cheating and take actions to prevent it (Salend, 2008; Villiano, 2006).

Preventing High-Tech Cheating

High-tech cheating is a concern associated with technology-based testing of which you need to be aware and address (Salend, 2008). High-tech cheating usually involves accessing unauthorized information such as notes, Web sites, e-mail, handheld devices, and cell phones. To address these types of academic dishonesty, you can prevent students from having access to these technologies when taking tests. You also can use classroom management software that allows you to monitor your students' use of technology during testing by viewing your students' screens to make sure they are not instant messaging or e-mailing others, or accessing saved files, Web sites, or unauthorized information during testing (Villano, 2006). In addition, you can make sure that your students do not have access to a wireless network during testing sessions.

Many test and quiz creation programs (see Appendix A) provide features that can minimize the likelihood of cheating. For example, these programs allow the creation of multiple versions of a test by randomly selecting questions from a test bank of questions entered by teachers. You also can reduce cheating by making online tests and quizzes only available to students at specific starting and stopping times.

Keys to Best Practice: Use technologies that have distracting features cautiously and on a limited basis (Salend, 2009; Skylar, 2007).

Limiting Distracting Features

Your students may find that some technologies contain features that are distracting to them. When this is the case, you should use these technologies cautiously and on a limited basis. For instance, while some students may need to take tests using a screen reader, others may be distracted by the audio sounds. You can limit the extent to which these distracting features interfere with the performance of students by providing students with headphones to foster hearing and attention, adjusting the volume, and eliminating unnecessary audio.

Keys to Best Practice: Use a range of test-creation software programs (Bouck, 2006; Edyburn, 2003; Salend, 2009; Thompson et al., 2005).

Fostering Teacher Preparation

Limited preparation and experience in using technology-based testing can be an obstacle for you and your colleagues. However, like Ms. Randolph and Mr. Smith, you can gradually introduce technology-based testing into your classroom by accessing a variety of resources, including other professionals and a range of test-creation software programs. These software programs can guide you in

- creating test and quiz items,
- aligning items to your state's and district's learning standards,
- developing multiple versions of tests and quizzes,
- administering tests via technology or on paper, and
- scoring and analyzing student performance in a range of formats (see Appendix A; Bouck, 2006).

For example, you can use the following programs:

- *TestTalker* (www.freedomscientific.com/LSG/products/testtalker.asp): A software package that includes a module to assist teachers in creating tests that are PDF files and a student module that reads tests to students and guides them in taking the test electronically
- *Premier Test Builder* (www.readingmadeez.com/education/TestBuilder.html): A program that facilitates the development of technology-based tests by providing tools that allow teachers to add their text, audio, and pictures to templates of the different types of questions, and then administer the tests to their students electronically via screen readers or other types of adaptive technologies
- *Marvel Math* (www.braillebookstore.com/marvel-math.htm): A program that guides teachers in creating and administering technology-based math tests that provide visual and auditory guidance and feedback via the use of animated characters and speech synthesis (Strobel, Arthanat, Fossa, Mistrett, & Brace, 2006)

As Ms. Randolph and Mr. Smith discovered, scanning and form-typing software also are available that can help you prepare tests and your students complete them (Thompson et al., 2005). Using these programs, tests are created as PDF files, or printed copies of tests are scanned into a digital format and then completed by students via a computer.

Resources are available to guide you in evaluating the accessibility of your technology-based tests (Skylar, 2007). Beddow et al. (2008) created the *Test Accessibility and Modification Inventory (TAMI)*, an evaluation tool that you can use to rate your computer-based tests. Hoffman, Hartley, and Boone (2005) offer guidelines for examining the extent to which PDF files are accessible to a range of students. Web sites that can provide teachers with feedback regarding the accessibility of their testing and instructional materials are presented in Appendix A.

SUMMARY

This chapter provided best practices for using technology-based testing, which you can combine with the best practices presented in Chapters 1 and 2 to enhance the validity and accessibility of your tests. You can use the reflectlist (see Figure 3.2) to review the main points presented in this chapter and examine the extent to which you are applying best practices for using technology-based testing.

Figure 3.2 Reflectlist for Using Technology-Based Testing

Reflect on your use of technology-based testing by rating the extent to which you are applying the following keys to best practices.

Keys to Best Practice	*Often*	*Sometimes*	*Rarely*	*Never*
I use technology to create and administer tests that enhance student motivation.	☐	☐	☐	☐
I use technology to tailor the administration of tests to the skill levels of my students so that the difficulty of each question depends on how they performed on the prior question(s).	☐	☐	☐	☐
I use technology to accommodate the individual testing schedule preferences of my students and colleagues.	☐	☐	☐	☐
I use technology to motivate my students by providing them with reinforcement and encouragement related to their responses and their testing behaviors.	☐	☐	☐	☐
I use technology to present tests and quizzes in academic game formats.	☐	☐	☐	☐
I use technology to provide my students with real-time feedback related to their test performance.	☐	☐	☐	☐
I use technology to help my students identify correct and incorrect answers, the types of errors they made, and the topics and concepts that they need to review.	☐	☐	☐	☐
I use technology to embed error minimization techniques into my tests and to motivate my students by limiting their test-taking errors.	☐	☐	☐	☐
I use a range of technologies that allow my students to make choices about the ways test items and directions are presented to them.	☐	☐	☐	☐
I consider presenting tests to my students using a range of screen- and text-reading programs.	☐	☐	☐	☐
I consider presenting tests to my students using text scanners and optical character reading (OCR) systems.	☐	☐	☐	☐
I consider presenting tests to my students using a range of low-tech devices.	☐	☐	☐	☐

Keys to Best Practice	Often	Sometimes	Rarely	Never
I consider presenting tests to my students with visual impairments using a range of technologies.	☐	☐	☐	☐
I consider presenting tests to my deaf and hard of hearing students using a range of technologies.	☐	☐	☐	☐
I consider presenting tests to my students who are English language learners using a range of technologies.	☐	☐	☐	☐
I consider providing my students with motor difficulties with alternate methods to access and use technology.	☐	☐	☐	☐
I consider whether my students' responses to test items can be facilitated by their use of voice-recognition and voice-activated systems.	☐	☐	☐	☐
I consider using a range of technologies to help my students who have difficulty responding orally or in writing to test questions.	☐	☐	☐	☐
I consider using a variety of technologies to aid my students in composing written responses to essay questions.	☐	☐	☐	☐
I consider allowing my students to use appropriate word processing and spell check programs to compose their essays.	☐	☐	☐	☐
I consider allowing my students to use word cueing and prediction programs to compose their essays.	☐	☐	☐	☐
I consider allowing my students to use electronic dictionaries, glossaries, and thesauri to compose their essays.	☐	☐	☐	☐
I consider allowing my students to use text organization, word usage, and grammar and punctuation assistance resources to compose their essays.	☐	☐	☐	☐
I consider allowing my students to use essay grading and feedback resources to compose their essays.	☐	☐	☐	☐
I am aware of and address the digital divide.	☐	☐	☐	☐

(Continued)

Figure 3.2 (Continued)

Keys to Best Practice	Often	Sometimes	Rarely	Never
I provide my students with numerous opportunities to use technology in daily classroom instructional activities.	☐	☐	☐	☐
I explicitly teach my students the skills they need to use specific technologies and to take technology-based tests.	☐	☐	☐	☐
I am aware of high tech cheating and take actions to prevent it.	☐	☐	☐	☐
I use technologies that have distracting features cautiously and on a limited basis.	☐	☐	☐	☐
I use a range of test-creation software programs.	☐	☐	☐	☐

- How would you rate your use of technology-based testing?
- What aspects are your strengths?
- In what areas do you need to improve?
- What steps can you take to improve your use of technology-based testing?

COMING ATTRACTIONS

Technology-based testing has great potential for helping students access testing programs. However, when using technology-based testing, you should identify and address potential concerns, evaluate the various technologies to see if they are appropriate for use by you and your students, proceed gradually, and consider whether the technology provides students with access to your tests without altering them. In addition to using the best practices for using technology-based testing presented in this chapter, you can enhance the effectiveness and inclusiveness of your teaching, testing, and assessment practices by

- teaching your students the effective study and test-taking skills and strategies they need to succeed on all of the types of tests they will take (see Chapter 4), and
- using a range of classroom assessments that supplement the use of testing to document student learning and inform your instruction (see Chapter 5).

4

Teaching Effective Study and Test-Taking Skills and Strategies

Ms. Reynaud watched her students closely when they took her tests. She noticed many of them seemed overly anxious and approached her tests in a disorganized and haphazard manner. She asked her students about the ways they studied and answered different types of questions. Based on her observations of and discussions with her students, she decided to teach them to use good study and test-taking behaviors.

Ms. Reynaud began by creating a brief survey that asked her students to identify the strategies they used to study and to take tests and used this information to make an instructional plan. She started providing students with study guides and having students work in groups to discuss what material was likely to be on tests. She had them work in groups to create flash cards, summaries, and drawings that they could use to study. She also led students in playing games like Jeopardy where students had to answer different types of test questions related to the topics and concepts their tests would cover.

Ms. Reynaud then spoke with students about her observations of their test-taking skills and strategies, and how the lack of such strategies was hindering their test performance. She explained that she wasn't pleased with their test scores and would like to help them do better by teaching them to use a test-taking strategy she called PIRATES that she learned when she was in college. She told her students the strategy would help them answer multiple-choice questions once they learned it, and then introduced the strategy and explained how she used the name, PIRATES, to remember it.

Prepare to Succeed

- Put your name and write PIRATES on the test.
- Allot time and determine an order for completing the parts of the test.
- Say something positive to yourself about the test and your performance.
- Start as quickly as possible and within two minutes.

Inspect the Test's Directions

- Read the directions very carefully.
- Highlight key words that tell you what to do and where to do it.
- Notice special requirements you need to follow.

(Continued)

(Continued)

Read, Remember, and Reduce to Answer the Test's Questions

- Read all parts of each question.
- Remember what we have been learning about.
- Reduce your answer choices by eliminating those that you know are incorrect.

Answer or Abandon

- Answer all questions you are sure of.
- Abandon those questions you are unsure of and mark them so you can turn back to them later.

Turn Back

- Turn back to all questions that were not answered.

Estimate When You Are Unsure of the Answer

- Avoid choices that contain absolute words.
- Choose the longest and most detailed choice.
- Eliminate choices that present similar information.

Survey the Test Before Handing It In

- Make sure you answered all of the questions.
- Stay with your first choice. (Holzer, Madaus, Bray, & Kehle, 2009)

After reviewing the strategy and the mnemonic for remembering it, Ms. Reynaud modeled its use while simultaneously explaining how she did it. She demonstrated how she used the strategy with several test items and highlighted the letters in the PIRATES mnemonic that she used to help her remember the steps involved. She then asked the students to compare the new strategy with the approaches they use to take multiple-choice tests.

Next Ms. Reynaud broke her students into small groups to learn the strategy. She gave each group cue cards to guide them in practicing and remembering the steps in the strategy. As the groups practiced using the steps with different multiple-choice items, Ms. Reynaud observed them and provided feedback. She also gave students opportunities to use the Test-Taking CD (Lancaster, Lancaster, Schumaker, & Deshler, 2006), a multimedia program including audio and video that teaches students to remember and use the test-taking strategy she had taught them.

Once Ms. Reynaud felt that her students had learned the strategy, she encouraged and reminded them to use it on their next test by embedding a picture of pirates on the test. During testing, she observed her students and periodically asked them to describe parts of the strategy to her to see if they were using it. She also examined her students' test performance and discussed their scores with them as well as whether or not they thought the test-taking strategy was helpful.

Because the strategy helped improve her students' test scores, Ms. Reynaud started teaching other studying and test-taking skills and strategies to them. In addition, she has held several meetings with her students' families to explain her testing and assessment practices and to solicit information from them about their children's study skills. She also reviewed with them suggestions about the ways families can help their children develop good studying and test-taking skills and posted these suggestions on her Web site.

- What study and test-taking skills and strategies do your students use?
- Are your students' study and test-taking skills and strategies effective?
- How did your students learn these skills and strategies?
- What additional skills and strategies do your students need to learn?

Like Ms. Reynaud's students, many students fail to use effective study and test-taking skills, which can hinder their test performance. As a result, rather than assuming that students know how to study for and take tests, many teachers and school districts consider teaching students ways to improve their test preparedness and test taking as important parts of their educational program for all of their students. The teaching of effective study and test-taking skills and strategies is especially useful for your students with special needs as well as your students who do well on classroom-based activities and assignments yet perform poorly on tests (Holzer et al., 2009; Meltzer, Roditi, Stein, Krishnan, & Sales Pollica, 2008).

Recognizing the importance of these skills and strategies, many school districts view the teaching of effective study and test-taking skills as important instructional goals for students with special needs and list them on students' IEPs and 504 accommodation plans (Strichart & Mangrum, 2010). This chapter offers you a variety of best practices for teaching effective study and test-taking skills and strategies to all of your students. Rather than teaching to the test, these best practices are designed to help your students improve their test performance. Specifically, this chapter addresses the following questions:

- How can I assess my students' study and test-taking skills and strategies?
- What effective study skills and strategies do I need to teach my students?
- What effective test-taking skills and strategies do I need to teach my students?
- How can I help my students who experience test anxiety?
- How can I teach effective study and test-taking skills and strategies to my students?
- How can I work with my students' families to support their children's use of effective study and test-taking skills?

HOW CAN I ASSESS MY STUDENTS' STUDY AND TEST-TAKING SKILLS AND STRATEGIES?

Keys to Best Practice: Assess your students' use of effective study and test-taking skills and strategies (Hughes, Schumaker, Deshler, & Mercer, 2002; Kirby, Silvestri, Allingham, Parrila, & La Fave, 2008; Rozalski, 2007; Songlee, Miller, Tincani, Sileo, & Perkins, 2008; Weinstein, Palmer, & Shulte, 2002).

Assessing Students' Study and Test-Taking Skills and Strategies

Like Ms. Reynaud, you can use several different techniques to assess your students' use of effective study and test-taking skills and strategies (Kirby et al., 2008). You can gather information about your students' use of test-taking strategies by observing them during testing and examining their answer sheets for evidence of the effective use of these techniques (Songlee et al., 2008). During and after testing, you can ask students to identify the test-taking strategies they use by asking them, "What are you doing now?" "How did you approach this question?" and "What things did you do to arrive at that answer?" You can encourage students to reflect on the extent to which their effort and motivation affected their test performance and helped them succeed on the test and whether the test covered the things they studied and contained the types of questions they anticipated (Rozalski, 2007).

A range of assessment tools designed to measure students' knowledge and use of study and test-taking strategies is available (see Figure 4.1). These assessment tools ask students to examine their academic behaviors related to their attitude, motivation, time management, studying, and test-taking skills (Weinstein, Palmer, & Shulte, 2002). You also can create your own survey to assess your students and use or modify the one presented in Figure 4.2. For students who have difficulty reading, you may need to read the survey items to them. You can modify these surveys for your students by simplifying the language, phrasing items in a yes-no or true-false format and using pictorials to support the understanding of items.

Keys to Best Practice: Use assessment data to plan and evaluate your study and test-taking skills and strategies instruction (Hughes et al., 2002; Kirby et al., 2008; Rozalski, 2007; Weinstein et al., 2002).

Based on the assessment results, you can determine which study and test-taking skills and strategies your students need to develop and then plan instruction accordingly. You can use these assessment techniques to evaluate the success of your instruction in helping your students learn to use effective study and test-taking skills.

Figure 4.1   Web Sites Related to Assessing and Teaching Study and Test-Taking Skills

Assessing Study and Test-Taking Skills

Prentice Hall's Student Success (www.prenhall.com/success/StudySkl/ssa.html)

Columbia Basin College (http://134.39.200.118/cbc/success/study_skill_assessment.cfm)

Cook Counseling Center (www.ucc.vt.edu/studyskills/ssaform.htm)

Online Advising and Educational Planning (www.wwcc.edu/student_services/online_adv/success/study_skill_assessment.cfm)

Learning Center (www.humboldt.edu/~learning/test_taking_survey.php)

Teaching Study and Test-Taking Skills

How to Study (www.howtostudy.org)

Mind Tools (www.mindtools.com/memory.html)

TestTakingTips.com (www.testtakingtips.com)

Test-taking Strategies (ccc.byu.edu/learning/strategy.php)

Study Guides and Strategies (www.studygs.net)

How-to-Study.com (www.how-to-study.com)

Socrato.com (www.socrato.com)

Figure 4.2   Sample Study and Test-Taking and Strategies Skills Assessment

Please choose the rating that best describes the skills and strategies you use to study for tests.

Study Skills and Strategies	I do this ALL of the time	I do this MOST of the time	I do this SOME-TIMES	I NEVER do this
I know what topics and concepts will be covered on tests.	☐	☐	☐	☐
I know what types of questions will be on tests.	☐	☐	☐	☐
I know how many points the different types of questions are worth.	☐	☐	☐	☐
I work with others to study for tests.	☐	☐	☐	☐
I create a schedule that helps me study for tests.	☐	☐	☐	☐
I study in short blocks of time and take frequent breaks.	☐	☐	☐	☐
I avoid cramming and stop studying the day before the test.	☐	☐	☐	☐
I establish specific goals for each study session.	☐	☐	☐	☐
I study the most difficult things first.	☐	☐	☐	☐
I study in a quiet and comfortable place that helps me to concentrate.	☐	☐	☐	☐
I have all the materials I need to study.	☐	☐	☐	☐
I develop an outline to identify important information from the materials I need to study.	☐	☐	☐	☐
I highlight key points and the relationships between concepts and topics.	☐	☐	☐	☐
I play games to review important content and skills.	☐	☐	☐	☐
I create word files or flash cards to practice vocabulary, formulas, and lists.	☐	☐	☐	☐
I use a variety of memory aids and mnemonic devices to remember important content and recall facts.	☐	☐	☐	☐
I try to predict which questions will be on the test.	☐	☐	☐	☐
I take practice tests.	☐	☐	☐	☐
I conclude each study session by creating summaries and visual aids of the key points to be remembered.	☐	☐	☐	☐
I sleep well the night before the test.	☐	☐	☐	☐
I eat healthy foods on the day of the test.	☐	☐	☐	☐

(Continued)

Figure 4.2 (Continued)

Please choose the rating that best describes the skills and strategies you use to take tests.

Test-Taking Skills and Strategies	I do this ALL of the time	I do this MOST of the time	I do this SOME-TIMES	I NEVER do this
I arrive on time to take tests.	☐	☐	☐	☐
I bring all the materials I need to take tests.	☐	☐	☐	☐
I feel relaxed when taking tests.	☐	☐	☐	☐
I feel confident and positive when taking tests.	☐	☐	☐	☐
I concentrate and stay focused when taking tests.	☐	☐	☐	☐
I listen carefully to the teacher's introduction of the test and directions.	☐	☐	☐	☐
I write my name and other required personal information on tests.	☐	☐	☐	☐
I list important information, definitions, formulas, dates, and names that I am likely to use throughout the test as soon as the test is distributed.	☐	☐	☐	☐
I jot down memory clues and drawings to remember important things.	☐	☐	☐	☐
I scan tests to identify the number and types of questions.	☐	☐	☐	☐
I scan tests to identify the point values and weights associated with each item and section.	☐	☐	☐	☐
I create a plan for working on the test.	☐	☐	☐	☐
I work initially on easier items.	☐	☐	☐	☐
I read the directions and questions carefully.	☐	☐	☐	☐
I highlight important parts of the directions and items.	☐	☐	☐	☐
I pay close attention to parts of the test that have been highlighted.	☐	☐	☐	☐
I ask questions and seek clarification if I do not understand the directions or the questions.	☐	☐	☐	☐

Test-Taking Skills and Strategies	I do this ALL of the time	I do this MOST of the time	I do this SOME-TIMES	I NEVER do this
I look for and use word, grammatical, pictorial, and content clues.	☐	☐	☐	☐
I talk to myself to figure out and plan answers.	☐	☐	☐	☐
I use scrap paper to figure out and plan answers.	☐	☐	☐	☐
I stick with my first answer when I am not sure of the correct answer.	☐	☐	☐	☐
I answer all questions unless there is a penalty for incorrect answers.	☐	☐	☐	☐
I guess by using reasoning and cues available on the test.	☐	☐	☐	☐
I eliminate obviously incorrect answers.	☐	☐	☐	☐
I check over my answers before handing in the test.	☐	☐	☐	☐
I use test-taking learning strategies.	☐	☐	☐	☐
I reflect on my use of test-taking strategies after a test has been returned.	☐	☐	☐	☐

When Working on Multiple-Choice Questions

	I do this ALL of the time	I do this MOST of the time	I do this SOME-TIMES	I NEVER do this
I anticipate the answer prior to reading all of the answer options.	☐	☐	☐	☐
I cross out obviously incorrect choices, carefully consider the other available choices, and choose the choice that is most complete and inclusive.	☐	☐	☐	☐
I paraphrase the question's stem when I am not sure of which choice to select.	☐	☐	☐	☐
I approach each option as a true-false statement when I am not sure of which choice to select.	☐	☐	☐	☐
I eliminate choices that present similar or equivalent information.	☐	☐	☐	☐
I choose the option that is longer and more detailed when I am not sure of which choice to select.	☐	☐	☐	☐

(Continued)

Figure 4.2 (Continued)

Test-Taking Skills and Strategies	I do this ALL of the time	I do this MOST of the time	I do this SOME-TIMES	I NEVER do this
I select options such as *All of the above* or *None of the above* when I am not sure of which choice to select.	☐	☐	☐	☐
I select one of the options that offers contradictory answers when I am not sure of which choice to select.	☐	☐	☐	☐
I select an option that offers numbers that represent the middle range rather than the extremes when I am not sure of which choice to select.	☐	☐	☐	☐

When Working on Matching Questions

	I do this ALL of the time	I do this MOST of the time	I do this SOME-TIMES	I NEVER do this
I review both columns in matching items to get an overview of the choices in each column and to determine their relationships.	☐	☐	☐	☐
I determine whether each column has an equal number of choices and if choices can be used only once.	☐	☐	☐	☐
I read the initial choice in the left-hand column, examine the entire list in the right-hand column, and find the appropriate match in the right-hand column.	☐	☐	☐	☐
I mark choices that have been used so I can see the remaining choices.	☐	☐	☐	☐
I work on the easiest pairs first.	☐	☐	☐	☐
I avoid guessing until most of the pairs have been matched.	☐	☐	☐	☐

When Working on True-False Questions

	I do this ALL of the time	I do this MOST of the time	I do this SOME-TIMES	I NEVER do this
I identify the type of true-false item I am being asked to answer.	☐	☐	☐	☐
I examine all parts of the statements.	☐	☐	☐	☐
I look for and use key words.	☐	☐	☐	☐
I mark a statement as false if any part of the statement is false or incorrect.	☐	☐	☐	☐
I realize that longer statements that contain specific details tend to indicate that a statement is true.	☐	☐	☐	☐

Test-Taking Skills and Strategies	I do this ALL of the time	I do this MOST of the time	I do this SOME-TIMES	I NEVER do this
I realize that statements that include a justification or a reason usually are false.	☐	☐	☐	☐
When statements are presented in the negative, I eliminate the negative words, decide if the revised statement is true, and then determine whether the original statement is true or false.	☐	☐	☐	☐
I guess true if I do not know the answer and there is no penalty for incorrect answers.	☐	☐	☐	☐

When Working on Sentence Completion Questions

I examine the number and length of the blanks provided.	☐	☐	☐	☐
I use the grammatical structure of the item to help me determine the missing word.	☐	☐	☐	☐
I examine the item to determine whether the correct answer is singular or plural.	☐	☐	☐	☐
I choose an answer that is logical and consistent with the statement of the question.	☐	☐	☐	☐
I evaluate my answers in terms of grammar, logic, and content.	☐	☐	☐	☐
I convert sentence completion statements into questions.	☐	☐	☐	☐
I write a descriptive answer and use synonyms when I do not know the exact word or phrase or the correct spelling.	☐	☐	☐	☐

When Working on Essay Questions

I make a plan for answering essay questions.	☐	☐	☐	☐
I determine if there are choices in answering essay questions.	☐	☐	☐	☐
I work on the easiest questions first.	☐	☐	☐	☐
I allot an equal amount of time for each question.	☐	☐	☐	☐
I examine important words and terms in the directions.	☐	☐	☐	☐
I jot down key terminology and concepts.	☐	☐	☐	☐
I make drawings to show relationships among concepts and topics.	☐	☐	☐	☐

(Continued)

Figure 4.2 (Continued)

Test-Taking Skills and Strategies	I do this ALL of the time	I do this MOST of the time	I do this SOME-TIMES	I NEVER do this
I create an outline of my answer.	☐	☐	☐	☐
I paraphrase the essay question as the topic sentence of my introductory paragraph.	☐	☐	☐	☐
I determine a logical sequence for my answer.	☐	☐	☐	☐
I write paragraphs so that they address main points followed by supporting information and details.	☐	☐	☐	☐
I have clear transitions from sentence to sentence and paragraph to paragraph.	☐	☐	☐	☐
I provide examples and cite specific information to support my perspectives, arguments, and statements.	☐	☐	☐	☐
I conclude my answer with a summary of the main points and an indication of why they are important.	☐	☐	☐	☐
I highlight key information embedded in sentences or paragraphs.	☐	☐	☐	☐
I present related points as bulleted or numbered lists.	☐	☐	☐	☐
I use a general statement to qualify my answer when I am unsure of a specific fact.	☐	☐	☐	☐
I proofread my answers for clarity, organization, completeness, legibility, spelling, and grammar.	☐	☐	☐	☐
I put down an outline and key points rather than leaving the question blank.	☐	☐	☐	☐
I tell my teacher how I would have elaborated on my answers if I had more time.	☐	☐	☐	☐
I show all of my work on math and science tests.	☐	☐	☐	☐
I use specific learning strategies to answer essay questions.	☐	☐	☐	☐

WHAT EFFECTIVE STUDY SKILLS AND STRATEGIES DO MY STUDENTS NEED TO LEARN?

Your students are more likely to perform up to their capabilities if they study for their tests. Therefore, you can help them learn a variety of effective skills and strategies to enhance their test preparation, studying, and memory.

Keys to Best Practice: Help your students learn to anticipate the content that will likely be covered on the test and the types of questions that will make up the test (Educational Testing Service, 2005; Meltzer et al., 2008; Rozalski, 2007; Strichart & Mangrum, 2010; Walker & Schmidt, 2004).

Effective Test Preparation Skills and Strategies

Prior to studying, effective test takers do several things to prepare to study. They make a focused effort to anticipate the content that will likely be covered on tests and the type(s) of questions that will appear on tests. You can help your students learn to do this and focus their studying by employing the following strategies:

- Provide them with an overview of the purpose and format of the test that includes the content, topics, and concepts to be covered on the test, the number of questions on the test, the item types and directions, the time they have to complete the test, and the scoring and the completeness of the responses required.
- Create study guides, review sheets, vocabulary lists, and outlines for students that highlight the material to be included on the test, the format of the test, the types of questions that will be on the test, and the resources students can use to help them study. A study guide template that you can use is provided in Figure 4.3.
- Devote class time to allow students to review their notes, assignments, textbooks, and reference materials to identify key vocabulary, content, and topics and to ask questions about the scope and breath of the content to be covered on the test.
- Create semantic webs that highlight and depict the relationship between important terms, concepts, and topics.
- Assign homework prior to tests that requires students to identify, review, and practice content that is likely to appear on the test.
- Give students time to review prior tests and quizzes covering similar content and examples of complete and correct student responses.
- Play academic games to review the content of a test as well as the format of questions. Like Ms. Reynaud, you can use games like Jeopardy to help students prepare for tests by having students answer multiple-choice, matching, true-false, sentence completion, and short essay questions related to test content.
- Provide students with a list of possible test questions (usually essay questions) that they should be prepared to answer on an upcoming test. You can then select a number of the questions from the list to appear on the test (Educational Testing Service, 2005; Meltzer et al., 2008; Rozalski, 2007; Strichart & Mangrum, 2010; Walker & Schmidt, 2004).

Figure 4.3   Teacher-Made Tests Study Guide Template

When is the test?

The date of the test is _____.

How much time should I spend studying for the test?

You should study at least ____ minutes/hours each day beginning on _____.

How many and what types of questions will be on the test?

How many points are sections worth?

The test will be made up of

___ Multiple-choice questions worth ___ points

___ Matching questions worth ___ points

___ True-false questions worth ___ points

___ Sentence-completion (fill in the blank) questions worth ___ points

___ Essay questions worth ___ points

___ Other types of questions worth ___ points

What topics will be covered on the test?

The test will cover the following topics:

❑   ❑

❑   ❑

❑   ❑

What vocabulary words should I know?

You should study and know the following vocabulary words:

❑   ❑

❑   ❑

❑   ❑

What concepts should I know?

You should study and know the following concepts:

❑   ❑

❑   ❑

❑   ❑

What materials should I study?

When studying for the test, make sure you review:

Textbook Chapters and Other Readings

Class Notes

Class Assignments

Homework Assignments

Web Sites and Online Information

How can I practice for the test?

Here are some practice questions:

1.

2.

3.

4.

What else can I do to prepare for the test?

Here are some other things you can do to prepare for the test:

☐

☐

☐

☐

Another way for your students to learn to identify the likely content covered on a test is to examine the amount of class time spent on it (Meltzer et al., 2008; Salend, 2008). Thus, your students can learn how to examine their notes, textbooks, and assignments to identify important material that appears repeatedly and to predict questions. You can teach your students to focus on cues from their teachers that indicate important content that may appear on tests, such as when their teachers repeat, review, ask questions, or write about specific content. Your students can be taught to pay close attention to material teachers mention in the days before the test. You also can help students by reviewing material and learning objectives to be covered on the test as well as engaging in a discussion of the importance of the material to students. Your students should learn to ask about content that is likely to be on tests.

Keys to Best Practice: Provide your students with time to work in collaborative groups to prepare and study for tests (Fisher & Frey, 2008; Glenn, 2004; Michaelson & Sweet, 2008).

You can provide your students with time to work in collaborative groups to prepare and study for tests. Your students can work collaboratively to review notes and textbooks, predict possible questions, and teach and quiz each other on specific facts, terms, concepts, and topics. They can work together to develop study guides, flash cards, memory aids, and visuals that are related to the content of the test.

Keys to Best Practice: Help your students learn to use effective study skills and strategies (Brigham Young University Counseling and Career Center, 2008; Educational Testing Service, 2005; Glenn, 2004; Lambert & Nowacek, 2006; Meltzer et al., 2008; Strichart & Mangrum, 2010; Walker & Schmidt, 2004).

Effective Study Skills and Strategies

In addition to anticipating the content covered and types of test questions likely to appear on tests, teaching your students how to study can help them improve their test performance (Lambert & Nowacek, 2006). Specifically, you can help your students learn to use the following effective study skills and strategies:

- Estimate the amount of time needed to study and develop a checklist that outlines the length of study sessions and the material to be studied including its priority and level of difficulty. Use this information to create a manageable study schedule of short, spaced, and focused sessions that address reasonable amounts of information to be studied and include short breaks away from the study area.
- Start to study early with short review sessions. Plan a major study session early enough to obtain clarification and assistance about difficult material from teachers.
- Avoid cramming at the last minute and conclude studying the day before the test.
- Avoid scheduling study sessions too close to meals or bedtime.
- Establish specific goals for each study session.
- Focus initial study sessions on the most difficult content and topics.
- Seek a distraction-free, quiet, comfortable environment that is conducive to studying (keep in mind that this may not be possible for some of your students).
- Avoid clutter by having a wastebasket to discard scrap paper and other materials no longer needed.
- Gather and organize all the materials to be used in studying including notes, textbooks, class and homework assignments, handouts, readings, quizzes, reference books, paper, writing utensils, highlighters, and technology.
- Develop an outline to index important information from the materials listed above. Such an outline may contain main points and secondary points or

key questions and the corresponding pages from textbooks, class notes, quizzes, classroom and homework assignments, and worksheets that address these points and topics.

- Highlight key points and the relationships between concepts and topics and create summaries and visual aids.
- Create and play games that foster the review and practice important material and skills.
- Use word files or flash cards to practice and remember content-related terminology, formulas, and lists.
- Predict test questions and practice taking tests using possible test questions, homework assignments, and textbook learning exercises.
- Study with others and teach material to a classmate, a friend, or a relative.
- Conclude each study session by creating written or audio summaries of the key points to be remembered. Compare these summaries with notes and textbooks, noting and resolving any differences (Brigham Young University Counseling and Career Center, 2008; Educational Testing Service, 2005; Glenn, 2004; Lambert & Nowacek, 2006; Meltzer et al., 2008; Strichart & Mangrum, 2010; Walker & Schmidt, 2004).

Keys to Best Practice: Help your students learn to use a variety of effective methods and mnemonic devices to develop their memory of test content (Meltzer et al., 2008; Mind Tools, 2008; Rozalski, 2007; Strichart & Mangrum, 2010; Terrill, Scruggs, & Mastropieri, 2004; Willingham, 2009).

Effective Memory Skills and Strategies

Studying for and taking tests require students to remember important material and quickly recall facts. Therefore, it is important to teach your students to use a variety of effective methods and mnemonic devices to develop their memory of test content such as the following:

- *Pictorials:* Your students can devise vocabulary picture cards, which include key terms to be studied paired with their definitions and pictorials depicting them. For example, to remember the definition of *stalagmite,* your students can create an index card containing a drawing of it with its definition.
- *Mental Visualization:* Your students can remember important concepts and terms by associating them with a mental image or symbol of the content. When using visualization, your students should be encouraged to create positive, pleasant, colorful, and three-dimensional images, as these qualities make the images more realistic and memorable. Memory of images can be enhanced by adding movement, appropriate humor, smells and sound, and exaggerating important parts.
- *Visual Associations:* Your students remember related words and concepts by using visual associations depicting these relationships, such as having two or more conflicting concepts collide, viewing similar concepts as joined together, placing sequentially related concepts in a staircase or their proper sequence, or linking related concepts by having them rotate around each other on a merry-go-round.

- *Key Word Method:* Your students prompt their memory of key vocabulary by linking these terms with a word that sounds similar to an easy-to-remember drawing or graphic of the key word and its definition. For instance, your students can learn the vocabulary word *Sauro* (lizard) by linking it to the key word *saw* and a drawing of a lizard sawing a log.
- *Stories:* Your students create brief stories with words and images that trigger their memory of sequential lists of related information or important concepts.
- *Loci:* Your students use images of familiar locations to prompt their memory of specific information or events. For example, your students can foster their memory of George Washington Carver, who discovered over 300 uses of peanuts, by imagining him eating peanuts in Washington, D.C.
- *Acronyms:* Your students recall important material by creating a memorable word or phrase based on the first letter of the words or phrases to be remembered. For example, your students can create *HOMES* as an acronym to prompt their memory of the names of the different Great Lakes or use the name *Roy G. Biv* to remember the colors of the light spectrum.
- *Acrostics:* Your students create a sentence based on the first letter of the information to be memorized or the specific sequence in which a series of words or content need to be remembered. For example, your students can foster their memory of the order of the planets from the sun by remembering the sentence, *My Very Energetic Mom Just Served Us Nachos.*
- *Categorizing:* Your students trigger their memory of a series of key terms or information by sorting them into groups based on common traits and then memorizing each group. For example, to foster memory of the 50 different states, your students can create groups based on geographical locations and then focus their studying on each geographic category.
- *Rhyming and Music:* Your students create rhymes and music to aid their memory of specific content. For example, your students can memorize the spelling rule rhyme, *i* before *e* except after *c.*
- *Games:* Your students play a variety of games such as Concentration using flash cards related to the content that they need to memorize for upcoming tests (Meltzer et al., 2008; Mind Tools, 2008; Rozalski, 2007; Strichart & Mangrum, 2010; Terrill et al., 2004; Willingham, 2009).

WHAT EFFECTIVE TEST-TAKING SKILLS AND STRATEGIES DO MY STUDENTS NEED TO LEARN?

Enhancing your students' test-taking skills and strategies can help them foster their success when taking tests (Holtzer et al., 2009; Kretlow, Lo, White, & Jordan, 2008; Strichart & Mangrum, 2010). Therefore, you can help them learn to use effective general test-taking skills and strategies as well as those that are useful when answering specific types of objective and essay questions.

Keys to Best Practice: Help your students learn to use effective general test-taking skills and strategies (Brigham Young University Counseling and Career Center, 2008; Glenn, 2004; Hughes et al., 2002; Kretlow et al., 2008; Songlee et al., 2008; Tennessee Department of Education, 2008; Walker & Schmidt, 2004).

Effective General Test-Taking Skills and Strategies

Once students receive their tests, they can engage in a variety of general test-taking behaviors. These effective test-taking skills and strategies, which are useful for taking all types of tests, ask students to practice the following:

- They listen carefully to the teacher's introduction of the test including instructions and directions.
- They write their names and other required personally identifying information.
- They scan the test to identify the number and types of questions on the test as well as the point values and weights associated with each item and section.
- They perform a *memory dump* of important information, definitions, formulas, dates, names, and drawings that they are likely to use throughout the test and jot down memory clues and drawings to promote recall. As students work on the test, it may be helpful to write notes in the margins as well as explanations for answers (e.g., *I selected choice (c) because . . .*).
- They create a plan for starting the test and budgeting their time based on the amount of time they have to complete the test, the specific point values and weights of questions and sections, and the levels of difficulty of the questions. In general, it is most efficient to work initially on easier items and sections that are worth the most points and to avoid spending too much time and energy on any single question (unless it is worth a significant number of points; Glenn, 2004).
- They employ the strategy that many successful test-takers use of making three passes through the test based on levels of difficulty. The first pass involves students reading all items, responding to items they can answer easily, and placing an icon next to those items that they view as difficult (?) and very difficult (??). In the second pass, students answer those questions marked as difficult; they then respond to all very difficult questions during the final pass.
- They read all parts of the directions and items carefully to identify the (a) specific details (e.g., *answer two out of the three essay questions*); (b) types of answers they are asked to provide; (c) aids, resources, and assistance they can use; and (d) time, length, and space constraints. To assist students in doing this, they can learn to strategically highlight critical parts of test directions and items. Students should learn to pay close attention to aspects of tests that have been highlighted via use of *italics,* **boldface**, and CAPITALIZATION.
- They seek clarification regarding test directions and items, language they do not understand, or questions that can be interpreted in several ways.
- They look for and use word, grammatical, pictorial, and content clues. For instance, word clues such as *always* and *never* suggest extremes and often indicate incorrect answers; grammatical correctness such as subject-verb agreement, verb tense, and modifiers can assist students in determining the correct response. Additionally, sometimes content from one test item can assist in figuring out the correct answer to another question.
- They engage in self-talk and use scrap paper to figure out and plan responses.
- They stick with their first response when they are not sure of the correct answer and change answers only if they misread the questions or obtained new information about the question elsewhere on the test. When changing

answers, students should make sure that they erase their previous answers completely.

- They respond to all items including extra-credit and bonus questions, even if it means writing partial answers or guessing, rather than leave questions unanswered. When guessing, students should use reasoning and the cues available on the test and eliminate obviously incorrect answers. However, on tests where students are penalized for incorrect answers, they should learn to respond only to items that have a high probability of being correct.

- They review questions and check answers to make sure they are correct, complete, easy to read, and marked appropriately. Students can learn to note that an item or page has been reviewed so that they do not have to use additional time checking it again. Prior to handing in their tests, students should be encouraged to make sure that they have not inadvertently skipped items, steps, or parts of answers or mismarked their answer sheets. In addition, students should proofread their written answers to make sure that they are logical and sound correct, and that they have correctly rewritten answers originally composed on scrap paper. Students should determine if they should provide more information or revise their answers, check their spelling, grammar, punctuation, and their mathematical calculations.

- They use a range of test-taking learning strategies such as the ones presented in Figure 4.4 , and the PIRATES strategy Ms. Reynaud taught her students.

- They reflect on their use of test-taking strategies after tests have been returned (Brigham Young University Counseling and Career Center, 2008; Glenn, 2004; Kretlow et al., 2008; Songlee et al., 2008; Tennessee Department of Education, 2008; Walker & Schmidt, 2004).

Figure 4.4 Sample Test-Taking Learning Strategies

ANSWER *(Hughes, Schumaker, & Deshler, 2005; Therrien, Hughes, Kapelski, & Mokhtari, 2009)*

Analyze the action words: Read the question very carefully and highlight the key words.

Notice requirements: Highlight and mark the important requirements of the essay and rephrase the question in your own words.

Set up an outline: List the main points of the essay in an outline.

Work in details: Add important details and supporting points to your outline.

Engineer your answer: Write your essay by starting with an introductory sentence followed by supporting sentences related to the main points in your outline.

Review your answer: Check your essay to make sure that you have answered all parts of the question and edit your essay.

Solve It! *(Montague, 2006)*

Step 1. Read the problem for understanding. Students read the problem to understand the question and to identify clue words that are used to help students determine the correct mathematical operations to be used.

Step 2. Reread and paraphrase the problem. Students read the problems again to identify, highlight, and paraphrase critical information and cross out irrelevant information and facts. Students start to determine what mathematical process and units should be used to answer the questions.

Step 3. Visualize and draw the problem. Students visualize the problem and draw a representation of the critical information provided to them.

Step 4. Hypothesize a plan and write the problem. Students hypothesize and write the steps in solving the questions in their sequence and list the appropriate signs.

Step 5. Estimate the answer. Prior to solving the question, students estimate the answer and examine the reasonableness of their estimate.

Step 6. Compute and *solve the problem.* Students solve the problem using the sequential steps they listed in Step 4.

Step 7. Check the answer. Students check their work and compare their answer with their estimate.

DETER *(Strichart & Mangrum, 2010)*

D Read the **Directions**. Ask for explanations of the directions or words you do not understand

E Examine the whole test to see how much you have to do.

T Decide how much **Time** to you should allot to each test question.

E Answer the **Easiest** questions first.

R Review your answers to make sure you did your best and answered all required questions.

SEWERS *(Rozalski, 2007)*

Sign your name to the test.

Examine the test and estimate how long you think it will take you to complete it.

Write down any mnemonics, memory aids, and important content that you have memorized.

Exhale and focus.

Read the instructions carefully. Highlight important parts of the directions.

Survey the whole test before turning it in.

DREAMS *(Yell & Rozalski, 2008)*

Directions must be read carefully. Look for keywords to identify what you are being asked to do. Keywords include *best, none, never, all,* and *always.*

Read all answers before choosing your answer.

Easy questions should be answered first. Skip the hard questions until you finish answering the easy ones.

Absolute qualifiers are usually false. Absolute qualifiers include *no, none, never, only, every, all, always.*

Mark questions as you read them. Cross out the ones you have answered. Place a star next to the questions that are difficult for you and return to them after you have answered all of the easier questions.

Similar and absurd options can usually be eliminated.

Although the general test-taking strategies just discussed are relevant for all types of test questions, learning unique effective skills and strategies for answering objective test questions and essay questions can aid students' test performance. In other words, your students need to learn to use a variety of test-taking skills and strategies that are appropriate for the different types of items they are likely to encounter on tests.

Keys to Best Practice: Help your students learn to use effective test-taking skills and strategies for answering multiple-choice items (Brigham Young University Counseling and Career Center, 2008; Glenn, 2004; Hughes et al., 2002; Kretlow et al., 2008; Meltzer et al., 2008; Strichart & Mangrum, 2010; Songle et al., 2008).

Effective Test-Taking Skills and Strategies for Multiple-Choice Items

Your students can learn to use effective test-taking skills and strategies that will help them answer multiple-choice items (Kretlow et al., 2008; Songlee et al., 2008; Strichart & Mangrum, 2010). When working on multiple-choice items, it is often best to read the item and anticipate the answer before examining all of the answer options. If their anticipated answer is not one of the answer choices, students should learn to eliminate and cross out obviously incorrect choices, to carefully consider the other available choices, and to choose the one that is most complete and inclusive. When students are not sure of which answer to select, it may help them to paraphrase the question's stem or to approach each choice as a true-false statement.

Your students can be taught how to identify the most likely correct response choices as well as ways to eliminate the choices that are least likely to be correct, such as those that present similar or equivalent information. Thus, when students are unsure of which choice to select, they can learn that the correct answer is most likely to be one of the options that

- is unusually long and detailed,
- contains language that is found in the stem or wording that is similar to the language used by teachers or in the textbook,
- is phrased as *All of the above* or *None of the above* (especially when two or more choices seem correct or incorrect),
- presents information that contradicts the other choices (when two choices offer opposite information, the correct choice is usually one of them),
- does not contain absolute words (i.e., always, all, never), and
- offers numbers that represent the middle range rather than the extremes.

Occasionally, multiple-choice tests are machine graded and require students to record responses in a grid on a separate answer sheet. To ensure that students do not lose credit because of the difficulties they may experience with this unique format, they should learn to

- use the correct writing tool;
- mark completely the grid that indicates the response;
- erase changes or mistakes thoroughly;
- fill in only one answer grid per item;
- check to see that the question numbers correspond to the numbers on the answer sheet;
- fold test pages and position the answer sheet so that only one page appears;
- check page numbers, especially when moving on to a new page; and
- check to see if the answer sheets have more than one side.

Keys to Best Practice: Help your students learn to use effective test-taking skills and strategies for answering matching items (Brigham Young University Counseling and Career Center, 2008; Meltzer et al., 2008; Strichart & Mangrum, 2010).

Effective Test-Taking Skills and Strategies for Matching Items

Your students can engage in a variety of test-taking skills and strategies to improve their performance on matching items (Brigham Young University Counseling and Career Center, 2008; Meltzer et al., 2008; Strichart & Mangrum, 2010). They should learn to initially review both columns in matching items to get an overview of the choices in each column as well as to determine their relationships. Students also should identify whether each column has an equal number of choices and if choices can be used only once. Many students find it helpful to work in an organized manner that involves

(1) reading the initial choice in the left-hand column,

(2) examining the entire list in the right-hand column,

(3) finding the match in the right-hand column,

(4) highlighting choices (e.g., crossing out) that have been used so that they can see the remaining choices, and

(5) reviewing all matches.

Since an incorrect initial match can increase the number of errors, your students should learn to work on the easiest choices first and avoid guessing until most of the pairs have been matched.

Keys to Best Practice: Help your students learn to use effective test-taking skills and strategies for answering true-false items (Brigham Young University Counseling and Career Center, 2008; Glenn, 2004; Strichart & Mangrum, 2010; Walker & Schmidt, 2004).

Effective Test-Taking Skills and Strategies for True-False Items

Many students experience problems answering true-false items. Your students can minimize these difficulties by learning to use the following strategies:

- Identify the type of true-false items they are asked to answer.
- Examine all parts of the statement and mark a statement as false if any part of the statement is false or incorrect.
- Look for *specific determiners* within true-false items, which are words that vary, qualify, limit, or provide the conditions and context associated with statements. When statements contain absolute words that imply that the statement is extreme or true 100% of the time, such as *no, never, none, every, always,*

every, entirely, only, all, best, worst, absolutely, and *certainly,* the statement is usually false. Conversely, the use of qualifiers that moderate statements, such as *sometimes, generally, often, frequently, ordinarily,* and *usually,* typically suggest that a statement is true. However, when true-false statements do not include a specific determiner, students should select true only if it is always true.

- Recognize that longer statements that contain specific details tend to indicate that a statement is true and statements that include a justification or a reason usually are false.
- Examine the impact of negative words and prefixes on the meaning and truthfulness of statements. When statements contain negatives, many students find it helpful to eliminate the negatives, assess whether the revised statement is true or false, and then determine whether the original statement is true or false.
- Guess true if they do not know the answer and there is no penalty for incorrect answers, as teachers tend to include more true statements than false statements on their tests (Brigham Young University Counseling and Career Center, 2008; Glenn, 2004; Strichart & Mangrum, 2010; Walker & Schmidt, 2004).

Keys to Best Practice: Help your students learn to use effective test-taking skills and strategies for answering sentence completion items (Brigham Young University Counseling and Career Center, 2008; Strichart & Mangrum, 2010).

Effective Test-Taking Skills and Strategies for Sentence Completion Items

Your students can employ a range of effective skills and strategies for working on sentence completion items (Brigham Young University Counseling and Career Center, 2008; Strichart & Mangrum, 2010). They should start by reading the statement and jotting down possible answers and then choosing the best answer. When students do not know the exact word or phrase or the correct spelling, they should attempt a descriptive answer and use synonyms since they might receive partial credit. Some students prompt their memory of the correct answer by converting these types of items into a question.

Sometimes a hint about the correct answer to this type of item is provided by examining the number and length of the blanks provided. Using this information, your students can learn that

- two blanks with no words between them often means that the correct answer is a two-word answer,
- two blanks separated by words can indicate that the correct answer is probably two different statements, and
- a long blank usually indicates that a phrase or a sentence is required.

Your students can learn how the grammatical structure of the item can aid them in determining the missing word, phrase, or number that correctly completes a sentence. For example, if *a* or *an* precedes the blank, students can use that information to figure out whether the correct answer most likely starts with a consonant or vowel. Examining the verb form can cue students to whether the answer is singular or plural. Students also should be encouraged to choose responses that are logical and consistent with the statement of the question and to evaluate their response in terms of grammar, logic, and content.

Keys to Best Practice: Help your students learn to use effective test-taking skills and strategies for answering essay questions (Brigham Young University Counseling and Career Center, 2008; Glenn, 2004; Meltzer et al., 2008; Strichart & Mangrum, 2010; Therrien, Hughes, Kapelski, & Mokhtari, 2009; Walker & Schmidt, 2004).

Effective Test-Taking Skills and Strategies for Essay Questions

Since essay questions require students to demonstrate their ability to organize, write, interpret, and apply information, preparation for answering these types of questions is critical for success (Therrien et al., 2009). When tests include more than one essay question, students should make a plan for answering all questions that includes working on the easiest questions first and allotting an appropriate amount of time for each question.

One technique that can help your students respond to a series of essay questions involves using a three-step process (Brigham Young University Counseling and Career Center, 2008; Glenn, 2004; Strichart & Mangrum, 2010; Walker & Schmidt, 2004). In the first step, students

- examine critical terminology in the directions to determine what they are being asked to do (the meanings of direction words typically used in essay questions are presented in Figure 4.5);

Figure 4.5   Direction Words for Answering Essay Questions

Essay Direction Words	What Students Should Do
Compare, contrast, distinguish, differentiate, delineate, relate	Focus the essay on the similarities and differences and relationships between topics, concepts, phenomena, individuals, groups, categories, etc.
Define, discuss, describe, examine, explain, justify, analyze, interpret, clarify	Focus the essay on the meaning of topics, concepts, phenomena, etc.
Summarize, review, state, synthesize, survey	Focus the essay on reviewing and summarizing information about topics, concepts, phenomena, etc.
Evaluate, prove, justify, debate, defend, argue, critique	Focus the essay on presenting and supporting a judgment or premise about topics, concepts, phenomena, etc.
Outline, list, diagram, trace, state, enumerate	Present the essay using outlines, webs, bulleted or numbered lists of main and supporting points coupled with brief descriptions or explanations

Source: Brigham Young University Counseling and Career Center (2008). *Test-taking strategies.* Retrieved July 8, 2008, from http://ccc.byu.edu/learning/strategy.php#6.; Rozalski, M. E. (2007). Practice, practice, practice: How to improve students' study skills. *Beyond Behavior, 17*(1), 17–23.

- determine if each question must be answered or if there are choices in answering questions;
- review questions and jot down key terminology and concepts and make drawings to show relationships among concepts and topics to be used in answering each question on scrap paper or next to the question;
- highlight information and drawings they have jotted down; and
- allot a specific amount of time for answering each item and reviewing your answers. In allotting time for each question, they should provide more time for more difficult questions, and record the amount of time to be devoted to answering specific questions next to each question.

The second step in the process involves your students

- placing the questions in an order from easiest to hardest and starting to work on the easiest questions first,
- rereading each question and adding new points and deleting unnecessary ones, and
- creating an outline of their response by identifying the important topics and key words and the sequence of their main points.

During the third step, your students use their outline as a guide and write their essay by

- paraphrasing the essay question or subquestions as the topic sentence of their introductory paragraph, which presents the main idea(s) and an overview of their response;
- refining and determining a logical sequence for their answer so that each subsequent paragraph addresses main points from their introduction followed by supporting information and details;
- establishing clear transitions from sentence to sentence and paragraph to paragraph;
- providing examples and citing specific information to support their perspectives, arguments, and statements; and
- concluding their answer with a summary of the main points and an indication of why they are important.

When appropriate, your students can learn to highlight key information embedded in their essays by underlining and presenting related points as bulleted or numbered lists. Students can learn that when they are not sure of specific facts, they should include a general statement that qualifies their answer. For instance, they can use the general term *during the early 20th century* instead of listing a specific year when they are unsure of the correct year.

Your students should learn to proofread their essays for clarity, organization, completeness, legibility, spelling, and grammar. Finally, since the scoring of most essay questions allows for partial credit, students should try to respond to each question in some fashion. Therefore, if they are running out of time, students should learn to put down an outline and key points rather than leaving the question blank. On math and science tests, it is important for your students to remember to show their work. When students run out of time, they can indicate this to you and note how they could have elaborated on their answers if they had more time. Specific learning strategies that students can use when answering essay-type questions are presented in Figure 4.4.

HOW CAN I HELP MY STUDENTS WHO EXPERIENCE TEST ANXIETY?

Keys to Best Practice: Help your students who experience test anxiety (Educational Testing Service, 2005; Tennessee Department of Education, 2008; Strichart & Mangrum, 2010; Walker & Schmidt, 2004).

Addressing Test Anxiety

Some of your students, particularly those with special needs, may suffer from test anxiety, which can interfere with their ability to concentrate and perform in testing situations. In addition to teaching your students to use the effective study and test-taking skills and strategies we just discussed, you can address their testing-related nervousness and anxiety by

- emphasizing the importance of arriving on time and taking a few minutes to relax and focus, rather than being too early, so that students avoid interactions with other students, which may intensify their anxiety (e.g., other students asking questions about what they studied, seeking the answers to questions that may or may not appear on the test, or spreading false rumors about tests);
- teaching and encouraging students to use relaxation techniques during testing;
- reminding students and encouraging them to focus on their past success and efforts and to periodically praise themselves during testing;
- helping students recognize that a reasonable level of nervousness may be helpful in fostering test performance;
- encouraging them to sit in a nondistracting area of the room (away from doors, windows, aisles);
- minimizing their fear of forgetting important information by teaching them to perform a memory dump, by listing critical points likely to be on the test as soon as the test is distributed; drawings and listings of mnemonic devices also can be used to prompt memory of important material;
- encouraging them to focus on one item at a time rather than being preoccupied with the whole test;
- teaching students to work on easier test items first so they can build their confidence, rather than becoming unnecessarily nervous about difficult items;
- embedding motivating and encouraging words and icons throughout the test as well as those that prompt students to relax (e.g., *You are halfway done. Relax, take a deep breath, and continue working*);
- encouraging students to ask questions and seek clarification during testing;
- having students complete tests in separate and comfortable locations and take breaks as needed;
- giving students additional time to complete tests and limiting your use of speed tests where the time limit affects students' performance;
- asking students how you can make the testing situation more pleasant and comfortable for them;

- using humor and minimizing competition;
- personalizing tests by phrasing items using students' names, interests, and experiences as well as popular characters, items, and trends;
- emphasizing the importance of getting a good night's sleep and eating healthy foods before the exam; you also can allow students to eat healthy snacks during the exam;
- prompting students to reflect on their use of strategies that helped them reduce their anxiety as well as those that they need to improve;
- reminding students that tests are only one way that you assess their academic performance and determine their grades;
- allowing students to take tests in collaborative groups and open book tests; and
- providing students with alternative assessment activities to demonstrate their mastery, such as those presented in Chapter 5 (Educational Testing Service, 2005; Strichart & Mangrum, 2010; Tennessee Department of Education, 2008; Walker & Schmidt, 2004).

HOW CAN I TEACH EFFECTIVE STUDY AND TEST-TAKING SKILLS AND STRATEGIES TO MY STUDENTS?

Keys to Best Practice: Explicitly teach effective study and test-taking skills to your students (Holzer et al., 2009; Hughes et al., 2002; Kretlow et al., 2008; Lenz, 2006; Songlee et al., 2008).

Explicitly Teaching Study and Test-Taking Skills and Strategies

Like Ms. Reynaud, you can help your students prepare for and take tests by explicitly teaching them the study and test-taking skills and strategies they need to learn, such as those presented in Figure 4.4 (Holzer et al., 2009). You do this by engaging in the following steps:

1. Select a skill or strategy that will improve your students' test performance.

2. Ask your students how they study for and take tests to identify the skills and strategies they use and to assess whether they are using these skills and strategies effectively and efficiently.

3. Guide your students in understanding the problems and difficulties associated with the ways they currently prepare for and take tests, and motivate them to learn new ways to study for and take tests.

4. Explain and describe the new skills and strategies including giving examples of their application and discussing their advantages over the strategies previously used by your students.

5. Solicit a commitment from your students to try to develop the new skills and learn the new strategies.

6. Describe and demonstrate the new skills and strategies, modeling and providing an explanation of the skill or each step in the strategy.

7. Prompt your students to verbally rehearse the skill and strategy.

8. Provide your students with numerous opportunities to practice the skills and strategies using appropriate materials.

9. Help your students understand the conditions associated with when to employ the skills or strategies.

10. Deliver feedback to your students regarding their mastery of the skills and strategies.

11. Assess your students' use of the skills and strategies.

12. Collaborate with your students to help them remember the steps of the strategy including providing them with self-monitoring checklists.

13. Obtain data on your students' test performance and examine the effectiveness of the strategy.

14. Help your students see the positive impact of the skills and strategies on their test performances.

15. Prompt your students to use the skills and strategies by creating tests that contain strategy-use reminders. (See Chapter 1.)

16. Promote generalization so that your students use the skills and strategies in studying for and taking all of their tests.

17. Collaborate with other professionals and family members so that they are aware of the skills and strategies, and model, prompt, and reinforce their use in different settings (Hughes et al., 2002; Kretlow et al., 2008; Lenz, 2006; Songlee et al., 2008).

Keys to Best Practice: Use a range of technologies to help your students learn effective study and test-taking skills (Lancaster et al., 2006; Saavedra, 2008).

Using Technology to Teach Effective Study and Test-Taking Skills

As Ms. Reynaud did, you can use technology such as the Test-Taking CD (Lancaster et al., 2006) to enhance your study and test-taking skills instruction. You can post test review materials, study guides (see Figure 4.3), important notes, and practice tests online, and provide students with links to Web sites that offer information and resources about study and test-taking skills and strategies (see Figure 4.1). Digital recordings of important classroom activities, teacher-directed presentations, class discussions, mini-lessons, and study and test-taking instructional sessions can be recorded and made available to students via CDs or audio and video podcasts (Saavedra, 2008). CDs and podcasts can include videos of students modeling and discussing the value of effective study and test-taking skills and strategies. You also can use digital resources such as the following:

- BrainCog (www.fablevision.com/braincogs/cog_product.htm), a CD-ROM presenting animated activities that help students learn to study for and take tests and quizzes

- Quizlet (www.quizlet.com), a Web site that offers a range of activities to help students learn vocabulary and information related to all subject areas
- Crammer Study and Sound System (www.leapfrog.com/gaming/crammer), a bilingual digital device that displays and orally presents individualized flash cards created on computers and test questions downloaded from the Web site
- Flashcard Exchange (www.flashcardexchange.com), a Web site that allows teachers and students to create and share flash cards and study guides and to play memory games
- Study Buddy (www.hamiltonelectronics.com/store/p/1084-Study-Buddy-card-reader-recorder-with-36-double-sided-re-usable-cards.aspx), a device that facilitates studying by allowing teachers and students to create flash cards that contain auditory and visual prompts
- Studystack (www.study.com), a Web site that provides students with access to a range of online studying activities such as flash cards and games across the curriculum
- Studyrails.com (www.studyrails.com), a Web site that helps students create personalized study plans, offers e-mail and cell phone study, and limits online distractions when studying

Your students also can visit such Web sites as Neuroscience for Kids: Memory and Learning (www.dls.ym.edu.tw/neuroscience/chmemory.html), Funbrain (www.fun brain.com/match), and Exploratorium (www.exploratorium.edu/memory/dont_ forget/index.html) to play online games designed to develop their memory skills.

HOW CAN I WORK WITH MY STUDENTS' FAMILIES TO SUPPORT THEIR CHILDREN'S USE OF EFFECTIVE STUDY AND TEST-TAKING SKILLS?

Keys to Best Practice: Collaborate and communicate with families to support their children's use of effective study and test-taking skills and strategies (Meltzer et al., 2008; Songlee et al., 2008; *Test-taking tips for parents*, 2008; Walker & Schmidt, 2004).

Your teaching of effective study and test-taking skills and strategies can be enhanced by involving your students' families (Meltzer et al., 2008; Songlee et al., 2008). Since families can be an excellent resource for helping their children develop the skills they need to be successful on your tests, you can collaborate and communicate with them in several ways. Via group and individual meetings, newsletters, handouts, e-mails, and postings on your class's Web site, you can share with and obtain information from them regarding their children's study and test-taking skills and strategies and ways to foster these skills.

Keys to Best Practice: Share information with your students' families about your testing and assessment practices (Meltzer et al., 2008; Tennessee Department of Education, 2008; *Test-taking tips for parents*, 2008; Walker & Schmidt, 2004).

Sharing Information About Your Testing and Assessment Practices

As part of your ongoing efforts to educate families about your classroom, you can have a meeting with your students' families focused on sharing information with them about your testing and assessment practices. For example, you can hold informational session(s) for families to address the following:

- Why assessment and testing are important
- What different assessment strategies you use and why you use them
- Why and when you give tests
- What your tests look like
- How you use information from tests and other assessments to evaluate and support student learning and to inform and differentiate your instruction
- What you do to help your students succeed on your tests (e.g., study guides and testing accommodations)
- What families can do to help their children study for and take tests
- What suggestions families have to help you improve your assessment, testing, and test preparation practices
- What questions families have about your testing and assessment practices (Walker & Schmidt, 2004)

You also can share with families examples of the materials and strategies you use to help their children study for and take tests, such as study guides (see Figure 4.3) and sample test-taking learning strategies (see Figure 4.4).

Keys to Best Practice: Obtain information from families about their children's use of effective study and test-taking skills and strategies (Meltzer et al., 2008; Tennessee Department of Education, 2008; Walker & Schmidt, 2004).

Obtaining Information From Families

You can obtain important information from families about their children's use of effective study and test-taking skills and strategies (Meltzer et al., 2008; Walker & Schmidt, 2004). You can ask your students' families to discuss their observations of their child's study habits and strategies as well as the ways they facilitate their child's test preparation and study skills. For instance, you can ask families to respond to the following:

- How do you and your child study for tests?
- What studying strategies do you and your child find most helpful?
- What difficulties do you and your child have in studying for tests?
- How can I help you and your child study for tests?

You can ask them to complete a survey assessing their children's use of a range of effective study and test-taking skills and strategies. For instance, you can adapt the survey presented in Figure 4.2 by asking family members to complete it based on their observations of their child's study and test-taking skills. Family members also can reflect on and develop their use of best practices for supporting their child's test performance (see Figure 4.6).

Figure 4.6   Checklist of Best Test Preparation and Study Practices for Families

✓ Check in advance that your child has completed all the class and homework assignments related to the content to be tested.

✓ Encourage your child to check with teachers about the content, format, and length of tests and the number, types, and point values of questions.

✓ Ask the teacher for sample and past test items and answers and have your child practice answering these questions.

✓ Note test dates in advance, mark them on a calendar, and try to limit your child's scheduled activities and appointments around the days leading up to tests.

✓ Inform teachers in advance of any important family events, health conditions, or holidays that may affect your child's test or class performance. Consider suggestions you can make for alternative assignments or scheduling of tests.

✓ Avoid the need to cram for tests by helping your child plan a reasonable study schedule that includes several shorter sessions, short breaks, and reasonable and focused study goals.

✓ Teach your child to gather all the materials needed for studying and to review materials provided by teachers (e.g., study guides, homework assignments, practice tests).

✓ Teach and encourage your child to use mnemonic devices to remember test content.

✓ Model for your child how to use effective test-taking strategies.

✓ Create a quiet, comfortable, well-lit study area for your child that is free of distractions.

✓ Motivate your child to study and perform well by conveying a positive, relaxed, and confident attitude toward studying and about tests.

✓ Establish reasonable expectations with your child.

✓ Acknowledge your child's efforts in preparing and studying for tests.

✓ Try to avoid being overly anxious and placing undue stress on your child.

✓ Encourage your child to finish studying early enough to relax for several hours and to get a good night's sleep before the test.

✓ Prepare healthy meals for your child to eat on the day of the test.

✓ Contact the teacher and school as soon as possible if your child is ill on the day of a test.

✓ Be supportive and encouraging if your child does not do as well as you would like.

✓ Talk with your child and your child's teacher to develop and evaluate a plan for helping your child succeed on tests and revise your efforts accordingly.

✓ After your child takes a test, reflect with your child on the test to identify successful strategies as well as ways to improve for future tests.

Source: Test-taking tips for parents (2008).

Keys to Best Practice: Provide families with guidelines and resources for fostering their children's use of effective study and test-taking skills and strategies (Meltzer et al., 2008; Tennessee Department of Education, 2008; *Test-taking tips for parents*, 2008; Walker & Schmidt, 2004).

Helping Families Foster Their Children's Use of Effective Study and Test-Taking Skills and Strategies

Information shared by you and your students' families can be used to develop and implement a plan to enhance their children's study and test-taking skills. An essential part of the plan is providing families with guidelines (see Figure 4.6) and resources (see Figure 4.1) they can use to support their child's use of effective study and test-taking skills and strategies. You can share these guidelines and resources with families by conducting a workshop for them, creating a handout or newsletter, or posting the information on your class's Web site including links to helpful online resources.

SUMMARY

This chapter provided best practices you can use to teach effective study and test-taking skills and strategies to your students. Rather than teaching to the test, these best practices allow you to help all of your students learn how to prepare for and succeed on the many tests they will be asked to take. You can use the reflectlist (see Figure 4.7) to review the main points presented in this chapter and to examine the extent to which you are applying best practices to teach effective study and test-taking skills and strategies to your students.

Figure 4.7   Reflectlist for Teaching Effective Study and Test-Taking Skills and Strategies to Your Students

Reflect on your teaching of effective study and test-taking skills and strategies to your students by rating the extent to which you are applying the following keys to best practices.

Keys to Best Practice	Often	Sometimes	Rarely	Never
I assess my students' use of effective study and test-taking skills and strategies.	☐	☐	☐	☐
I use assessment data to plan and evaluate the study and test-taking skills and strategies instruction I provide to my students.	☐	☐	☐	☐
I help my students learn to anticipate the content that will likely be covered on tests and the types of questions that will make up tests.	☐	☐	☐	☐
I provide my students with time to work in collaborative groups to prepare and study for tests.	☐	☐	☐	☐

(Continued)

Figure 4.7 (Continued)

Keys to Best Practice	Often	Sometimes	Rarely	Never
I help my students learn to use effective study skills and strategies.	☐	☐	☐	☐
I help my students learn to use a variety of methods and mnemonic devices to develop their memory of test content.	☐	☐	☐	☐
I help my students learn to use effective general test-taking skills and strategies.	☐	☐	☐	☐
I help my students learn to use effective test-taking skills and strategies for answering multiple-choice items.	☐	☐	☐	☐
I help my students learn to use effective test-taking skills and strategies for answering matching items.	☐	☐	☐	☐
I help my students learn to use effective test-taking skills and strategies for answering true-false items.	☐	☐	☐	☐
I help my students learn to use effective test-taking skills and strategies for answering sentence completion items.	☐	☐	☐	☐
I help my students learn to use effective test-taking skills and strategies for answering essay questions.	☐	☐	☐	☐
I help my students who experience test anxiety.	☐	☐	☐	☐
I explicitly teach effective study and test-taking skills to my students.	☐	☐	☐	☐
I use a range of technologies to help my students learn effective study and test-taking skills.	☐	☐	☐	☐
I use a variety of strategies to collaborate and communicate with families to support their children's use of effective study and test-taking skills and strategies.	☐	☐	☐	☐

Keys to Best Practice	Often	Sometimes	Rarely	Never
I share information with my students' families about my testing and assessment practices.	☐	☐	☐	☐
I obtain information from families about their children's use of effective study and test-taking skills and strategies.	☐	☐	☐	☐
I provide families with guidelines and resources for fostering their children's use of effective study and test-taking skills and strategies.	☐	☐	☐	☐

- How would you rate your teaching of effective study and test-taking skills and strategies to your students?
- What aspects are your strengths?
- In what areas do you need to improve?
- What steps can you take to improve your teaching of effective study and test-taking skills and strategies to your students?

COMING ATTRACTIONS

We have discussed best practices you can use to create and grade valid and accessible teacher-made tests (see Chapter 1), to provide your students with valid and appropriate testing accommodations (see Chapter 2), to use technology-based testing (see Chapter 3), and to help your students develop effective study and test-taking skills and strategies. You can use inclusive classroom assessments to supplement your use of testing, which we will discuss next.

5

Using Classroom Assessments

Ms. Locasio has been teaching her students about poetic devices. Using an interactive whiteboard, she reviewed the poetic devices they have learned so far and asked her students to use their wireless active responding clickers to rate their levels of understanding these poetic devices on a scale of one to three. By reviewing her students' responses, Ms. Locasio determined that the class was ready to proceed. She went on to identify and define several new poetic devices for the class. She simultaneously displayed the words of several poems on the interactive board and discussed the different poetic elements used. Periodically, Ms. Locasio asked students to use their clickers to respond to true-false questions about the poetic elements. The students also used their clickers to play a game, Name That Poetic Device, which asked them to identify specific poetic devices used in various poems. Based on a summary of the students' answers provided to her, Ms. Locasio quickly assessed student understanding and determined which students were ready to start writing poems using the different elements. She also used individualized student response data to identify the specific poetic elements she needed to continue to teach some of her students.

Ms. Leon worked with her students to develop an instructional rubric to evaluate their performance on their next assignment, a WebQuest titled Culture Quest. The goal of the Culture Quest was for students to understand, explore, and research the culture and customs of groups in the United States by visiting teacher-designated Internet sites, interviewing individuals, and gathering resources in the school's library and media center. Ms. Leon planned to have the class work in groups and each group was to select and study aspects of a culture of a group (e.g., art, music, symbols, and famous people) and create a Web site.

Prior to introducing the assignment to her students, Ms. Leon examined several WebQuests and instructional rubrics that were available online. Ms. Leon then met with her students to solicit their assistance in creating an instructional rubric for their Culture Quest assignment. First, she reviewed with them an example of an exemplary Web site developed by another class and discussed with them the features of the Web site that made it successful. Next, she showed them a Web site that needed improvement and discussed with them the features of the site that were lacking. Together, Ms. Leon and her students listed the ways in which the two Web sites differed and grouped them into three categories: content, design, and literacy skills.

Next, Ms. Leon divided the class into groups. She asked each group to create a set of brief statements that describe the specifics of one of the categories, and a scale for judging each of the statements in that category using four levels of performance. Each group then presented their statements and scale to the class and revised it based on the feedback they received from their classmates.

Ms. Leon then took the groups' four levels of performance and produced an instructional rubric, which she reviewed with the whole class. She asked the groups to examine the two Web sites a second time using the rubric and discussed how they would evaluate the Web sites. Confident that her students understood her expectations and how to use the rubric, she assigned students to their Culture Quest groups and told them she would evaluate their Web sites using the rubric. As students completed drafts of sections of their Web sites, Ms. Leon and peer reviewers gave them feedback using the rubric. When groups handed in their final products, Ms. Leon graded them using the rubric.

Since Ronald's IEP specifies his learning progress will be measured via alternate assessments rather than statewide testing, Mr. Shaw and the other educators worked with Ronald to develop a digital portfolio linked to statewide learning standards. When the class worked on measurement, Mr. Shaw used a digital camcorder to document Ronald engaged in various activities measuring ingredients for a recipe. These audio and video recordings of Ronald were then downloaded into Ronald's digital portfolio. Ronald's portfolio also included a digital observation of Ronald interacting with his peers during cooperative learning group activities and a digital story of Ronald's career preferences and transitional goals, which Ronald helped create and shared with the members of his IEP team.

- What classroom assessment strategies do you use to supplement your use of tests to examine your students' learning?
- How do you use technology to support your use of classroom assessments?
- How do you assess your students who do not participate in high-stakes testing programs?

In addition to using tests, it is important for you to use classroom assessments to evaluate your students' learning and inform your instruction. Classroom assessments involve the use of learning products associated with daily instruction to examine students' learning, document students' strengths and challenges, and evaluate the effectiveness of instruction. Classroom assessments have many advantages (see Figure 5.1), which make them an excellent way to link your assessment and instruction and to supplement your use of testing to examine your students' learning and your teaching success.

This chapter offers a variety of best practices you can use to implement classroom assessments to document and monitor your students' learning and inform your instruction. While classroom assessments can be implemented without the use of technology, many teachers like Ms. Locasio, Ms. Leon, and

Figure 5.1   Advantages of Using Classroom Assessments

- Links assessment and instruction
- Based on content from the curriculum and the instructional program
- Used on an ongoing basis
- Used to assess academic, social, and behavioral development
- Involves teachers and students in the assessment process
- Includes information about how students perform learning activities
- Helps students gain control over and insight into their own learning
- Promotes student motivation, self-reflection, and self-determination

Mr. Shaw are using technology to support their use of classroom assessments. For example, while you can use dry erase boards, different colored cards, and student gestures to implement active responding systems, technology-based active responding systems (clickers) are being used to provide teachers and their students with interactive real-time assessment systems. Therefore, this chapter provides technological strategies and resources that you and your students can use to foster the implementation of classroom assessments. Appendix B provides a list of Web sites to obtain additional information about the technology resources mentioned in this chapter. Specifically, this chapter addresses the following questions:

- How can I use classroom assessments to monitor the learning progress of my students?
- How can I use classroom assessments to implement performance assessment?
- How can I use technology to implement performance assessment?

Keys to Best Practice: Use a range of classroom assessments to monitor the learning progress of your students (Layton & Lock, 2008; Overton, 2009).

HOW CAN I USE CLASSROOM ASSESSMENTS TO MONITOR THE LEARNING PROGRESS OF MY STUDENTS?

Progress Monitoring

Classroom assessments can be particularly helpful in monitoring the learning progress of your students and making decisions about how to improve your instruction (Tomlinson, 2008). *Progress monitoring* refers to your conducting ongoing assessments to determine your students' learning progress and the effectiveness of your instructional program. Thus, assessment data are continuously collected over time and promptly analyzed to identify students who are progressing and ready for new instruction as well as those students who have not yet demonstrated mastery and need additional or revised instruction (Yell, Busch, & Rogers, 2007). A variety of classroom assessment strategies that you can use to monitor the learning progress of your students are discussed in the following sections.

Keys to Best Practice: Use curriculum-based measurement to assess your students' learning progress (Capizzi & Fuchs, 2005; Foegen, 2008; Hessler & Konrad, 2008).

Curriculum-Based Measurement (CBM)

You can use *curriculum-based measurement* (CBM) to continuously assess your students' learning progress and the effectiveness of your instructional

Figure 5.2 Sample Curriculum-Based Measurement Graph

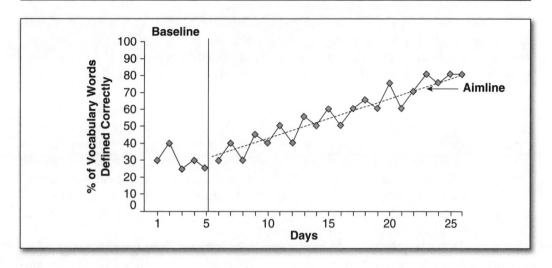

interventions (Capizzi & Fuchs, 2005; Foegen, 2008; Hessler & Konrad, 2008). CBM is a process involving repeated measurements of individual student progress in mastering content and skills directly related to the curriculum. For instance, you can use CBM to examine your students' progress in defining key vocabulary terms and the effectiveness of your instruction by repeatedly assessing your students' ability to define the key terms. Figure 5.2 contains a sample graph of CBM data.

CBM is an integral part of the *response-to-intervention* (RTI) method, a systematic and multi-tiered process that identifies students with learning disabilities as those students who do not respond to a series of research-based interventions (Fuchs & Fuchs, 2005). The use of CBM to formally implement RTI requires systematic policies, practices, and procedures related to delivering research-based instruction, determining aimlines based on norms for growth rates at various grade levels, and assessing student progress, and it is beyond the scope of this book (see Bender & Shores, 2007; Hoover, 2009; and Mellard & Johnson, 2007, to learn more about implementing the RTI process). However, you can adapt the CBM process to informally assess your teaching and your students' learning across the curriculum by considering the following steps.

Step 1: Examine your curriculum to determine the curricular content areas and skills to be assessed.

Step 2: Identify your assessment probe and the sample duration. Choose meaningful learning activities and tasks that are directly related to your curriculum to be your assessment probe. Also determine the sample duration by establishing the amount of time your students will have to complete the assessment probe. For example, an assessment probe for reading can involve your students reading aloud from their books or readers for a sample duration of 1 minute, and an assessment probe for social studies can be having your students define key terms during a sample duration of 10 minutes.

Step 3: Develop the materials you will need to implement your assessment probe and to deliver your instruction.

Step 4: Administer the assessment probe to establish a baseline. A baseline is a measure of the student's performance on the assessment probe prior to your teaching. It provides a standard that allows you to judge the effectiveness of your instruction. While the number of days to establish a baseline varies, generally you should allow at least three days.

Step 5: Determine an aimline. An *aimline* is a dotted diagonal line on your CBM graph that provides an estimate of the student's expected rate of progress from baseline measures to expected levels of mastery (see Figure 5.2). The aimline is individually determined based on the student's baseline data and learning strengths and challenges, as well as the levels of mastery you expect the student to attain and the length of time you plan to devote to instruction. It provides you and your students with a visual way to examine their learning progress and to judge the effectiveness of the instructional program.

Step 6: Deliver instruction and administer the assessment probe for each instructional session. You track the student's learning progress by providing instruction and then administering the assessment probe.

Step 7: Collect and graph student performance. Each time you administer the assessment probe, you graph the data—the number, percentage, or rate of the correct responses—using the following guidelines (see Figure 5.2):

- Place the assessment probe skill on the vertical ordinate (y-axis).
- Place the teaching sessions (days) in consecutive order on the horizontal (x-axis).
- Raise the zero point above the horizontal axis because it can be hard to see points on a line.
- Give your graph a title.
- Use solid vertical lines to indicate changes from baseline to intervention phases.
- Use a broken vertical line to indicate significant changes in your teaching.
- Use different symbols and unique connecting lines when graphing more than one data set.

Step 8: Examine the results to assess student learning progress and inform instruction. You can periodically examine the CBM data and compare it to the student's aimline to assess whether the student is making adequate learning progress. You also can use the data to inform your instruction and to compare the effectiveness of the different instructional strategies you have used. Thus, you can determine whether the student

- is making adequate progress and your instruction should be continued until mastery is established,
- has achieved mastery and is ready for more challenging instructional objectives, or
- is not progressing and needs adjustments related to the level of difficulty of the instructional objectives and the teaching strategies you are using.

Technology can facilitate the implementation of progress monitoring and CBM (Parette, Peterson-Karlan, Wojcik, & Bardi, 2007). You can use handheld devices and access various Web sites to create CBM assessment probes and to record, graph, analyze, and share your CBM data (see Appendix B). Wireless Generation (www.wgen.net) offers technology-assisted progress monitoring systems called mClass to assess students' reading and math progress and to record observations of and interviews with students to identify their thought processes. Your students can be taught to use software packages to graph, store, access, and reflect on CBM data regarding their learning and behavior. They also can use technology-based self-monitoring tools via PDAs that can be adapted for individual student via use of pictorial, tactile, and auditory prompts (Mitchem, Kight, Fitzgerald, Koury, & Boonseng, 2007).

Keys to Best Practice: Use active responding systems to conduct real-time assessments of your students' learning and to check their understanding of the content and skills you have taught (Barber & Njus, 2007; Beatty, Gerace, Leonard, & Dufresne, 2006; Horn, Schuster, & Collins, 2006; Maheady, Michielli-Pendl, Mallette, & Harper, 2002).

Active Responding Systems

You can use active responding to conduct real-time assessment of your students' learning progress and to check their understanding of the content and skills you have taught. After teaching new content, you can have your students respond actively by

- displaying colored cards to indicate their levels of understanding; for example, a green card can indicate a good understanding, a yellow card can indicate some understanding, and a red card can indicate limited or no understanding;
- responding chorally or in unison with gestures (thumbs up or down, OK sign, etc.) to short answer or true-false questions or stating their agreement or disagreement with specific statements and examples;
- writing answers on dry erase boards to questions or problems;
- completing exit tickets at the end of class where they write down their answer(s) to questions you have posed related to the content and skills you taught that day (Horn et al., 2006; Maheady et al., 2002).

As Ms. Locasio demonstrated, you also can use technology-based active responding systems, sometimes referred to as *clickers* or *classroom response systems*. These systems have the added advantage of making your classroom presentations more interactive, motivating, and effective. These wireless systems allow you to monitor student learning by having your students periodically respond electronically to factual, computational, conceptual, and comprehension questions; probes and quizzes; interactive activities; and poll, opinion, and review questions (Beatty et al., 2006). Thus, you can use these systems to have all of your students, not just the ones who raise their hands, answer objective questions (e.g., multiple-choice and true-false questions) and predict the outcomes of readings, word problems, and science experiments. Individual student and class-wide responses can be immediately tabulated and displayed so that you can use the data to assess your students' learning, guide your feedback, and adjust your instruction accordingly. For example, during her lessons on poetic elements, Ms. Locasio assessed her students' understanding of key points by asking them to respond to her questions via a wireless response system. She then used their responses to determine which students were ready to proceed to the next activity and to target her teaching for students who needed additional instruction. You can use these systems to make choices about whether to make the results available to students to provide them with prompt feedback.

These systems allow your students, especially those who are quiet or shy, to "silently" ask questions and let you unobtrusively send responses or provide feedback to individuals or groups of students. Like Ms. Locasio, you can use technology-based active responding systems to solicit feedback from your students concerning their mastery of content presented in class and to involve students in academic learning games. Additional information and resources related to the use of technology-based active responding systems are presented in Appendix B.

Keys to Best Practice: Use observations to assess your students' academic performance and classroom-related behaviors (Layton & Lock, 2008; Overton, 2009; Salend, 2008; Tam & Heng, 2005).

Observations

You can use observations to assess your students' academic performance and classroom-related behaviors (Salend, 2008; Tam & Heng, 2005). Observations can be conducted in a variety of ways. If the behavior has a clear beginning and end, you can use *event recording* to count the number of times the behavior occurs during the observation time. For example, you can use event recording to count the number of errors a student makes during reading or math and the number of times a student calls out without your permission during teacher-led activities. If time is an important feature of the behavior being observed, you can use *duration recording* to record how long the behavior lasts. For instance, you can use duration recording to assess the amount of time your students are on-task or the time it takes them to complete various academic tasks.

Observations are often presented as an *anecdotal record,* which is a narrative of the behaviors of students and teachers and the events that occurred throughout the observation. The narrative is then examined to identify your students' academic, social, and behavioral skills, your effective teaching behaviors, and the other classroom environmental variables that affect your students' behavior and learning. For example, you use a narrative observation to examine your students'

- appropriate and inappropriate behaviors;
- academic strengths and challenges;
- attitudes, effort, and self-concepts;
- attention and frustration levels;
- socialization with others;
- use of learning strategies;
- ability to understand and follow directions;
- idiosyncratic behaviors; and
- language, motor abilities, and speech habits.

When reviewing observation data, it is important for you to consider whether the student's behavior was consistent or whether it changed from activity to activity or over time.

In writing a narrative observation, you should use the following guidelines:

- State the date, time, and length of the observation.
- Briefly describe the activities and the physical setting in which the student was observed.
- Identify the students, teachers, and other professionals who are present while respecting their confidentiality.
- Provide an indication of the sequence and duration of events. You can do this by using such sequence words as *first, next,* and *then.*
- Report the nonverbal and verbal behaviors of the student as well as the responses of classmates and adults in observable terms so that you avoid making interpretations. For example, "Steven became angry and had a temper tantrum" makes an interpretation about Steven's behaviors. However, the statement "Steven rolled on the floor kicking and crying" presents the behavior without giving an interpretation.
- Avoid using adjectives and adverbs as they often lead to judgments and interpretations.
- Report information in a confidential manner.
- Try to write up the observation after it occurs.
- Be aware of your biases, mood, and other factors that may affect your observations.
- Observe over a period of time and vary the times and settings in which you observe.

In addition to using anecdotal records to document students' performance on a range of content areas activities, you can structure and report your observations by using teacher-made rating scales or checklists such as the one presented in Figure 5.3.

Like Mr. Shaw did with Ronald, you can use digital visual and audio recorders to make recordings over time of students performing various learning activities and classroom routines, engaging in learning strategies, and interacting with others in a range of classroom situations. For example, digital videos can be used to record your students

- discussing their learning goals throughout the year,
- demonstrating how they solve problems,
- identifying questions they have at the beginning of a unit of instruction and then answering them at the end of the instructional unit, and
- communicating with their families about their learning progress (Sprankle, 2008).

Digital observations can then be viewed by you and your colleagues and your students and their families to note academic, social, and behavioral progress and to identify the skills and behaviors that students have mastered as well as those in need of further instruction. They can help you identify effective instructional

Figure 5.3   Sample Observation Checklist

CHECKLIST TO EXAMINE STUDENTS' UNDERSTANDING OF NARRATIVE TEXT

Student: _____

Teacher: _____

Date(s): _____

Directions: Use the following system to record student behavior:

N = Student does not engage in the behavior.

B = Student is beginning to engage in the behavior.

D = Student is developing the behavior.

P = Student has proficiency in the behavior.

Support your notations with comments.

Narratives	Behavior	Date(s)	Comments
Names characters			
Describes the setting			
Identifies time/place			
Identifies problems			
Identifies solutions			
Predicts story outcomes			
Identifies mood			
Describes author's view			
States theme of story			

Source: From "Authentic Assessment Strategies," by K. Pike and S. J. Salend, *Teaching Exceptional Children, 28*(1), 1995, p. 16. Copyright © 1995 by the Council for Exceptional Children. Reprinted with permission.

strategies and other classroom stimuli and events that affect your students' learning and behavior. For example, you can use a series of digital observations of a student to

- identify and document appropriate and problematic behaviors;
- determine why, where, and when a student uses specific behaviors;
- identify the instructional, social, affective, cultural, environmental, and contextual antecedents and consequences that appear to lead to and maintain a student's behaviors; and

- plan appropriate interventions that address the purposes the behaviors serve the student to increase appropriate behaviors and decrease problematic behaviors.

Technology can aid you in conducting and communicating the results of observations (Edyburn & Basham, 2008). Handheld computers and PDAs can help you compose anecdotal records of the events that took place during an observation and record and graph real-time data about student behaviors and interactions. Technology-based observation systems designed to record and analyze real-time audio and visual observation data that can be used to assess your students' behaviors are presented in Appendix B.

Keys to Best Practice: Use academic games and technology-based educational games to assess student learning (Bouck, 2006; Cote, 2007; Mounce, 2008).

Academic Games and Technology-Based Educational Games

A creative and motivating way you can foster and assess student learning is through the use of academic games, including board games and movement-oriented games. Academic games allow you to monitor your students' learning progress by examining their responses to questions or activities that allow them to progress through the game. Because you control the content and levels of difficulty of the questions and learning activities, you can vary them to match the different skill levels of your students. When using academic games, it is important to make sure that your students do not become overly competitive and stimulated and that they understand the rules for playing the games.

It is beneficial if you foster collaboration among your students and minimize competition with others. You can do this by using common-goal games, whereby winning only occurs when everyone completes the game or achieves a goal. You also can promote collaboration by phrasing questions so they require students to consult their classmates and periodically having students change teams or places within the game. You can foster individual competition with oneself by using students' prior performances to increase the levels of difficulties of the questions they are asked to answer and to establish individualized time limits for answering speed-based questions.

You also can use technology-based educational games (Bouck, 2006). Using software programs and Web sites, you can create or have students access novel and motivating assessments across the curriculum that are presented via video, interactive whiteboard, PowerPoint, or collaborative game formats (Cote, 2007; Mounce, 2008). These programs and resources provide you and your students with several options so that the games can be adjusted to their preferences and skill levels. For instance, students can play these games alone or in groups, and you can tailor the levels of difficulty of the questions to your students' skill levels. These programs allow you to align the content of the games to your state's learning standards and your curriculum. They also can provide you and your students with immediate access to information on their performance, including the topics assessed and correct and incorrect responses. The following are examples of these technology-based educational games:

- *Gameshow Prep* (www.learningware.com), a software program that allows teachers to create television-style academic games related to their curriculum
- *Science.net*, a technology-based game in which students adopt the roles of journalists and write stories about science and technology for online magazines (Shaffer, 2007)
- *My Word Coach* (www.mywordcoach.us.ubi.com), a series of video games designed to teach and assess word vocabulary and spelling
- *DimensionM* (www.tabuladigita.com), a Web site that offers an immersive 3-D video game format that provides individual or groups of students with a series of real-world challenges designed to promote and assess their mathematics problem-solving skills
- *Mind Reading: The Interactive Guide to Emotions* (www.jkp.com/mindreading), a software package containing photographs and video and audio clips of different emotions that can be varied and presented to students as interactive games or quizzes to teach and assess students' understanding of a range of emotions (Lacava, Golan, Baron-Cohen, & Myles, 2007)

Additional resources that you can use to create and learn more about technology-based educational games to assess your students' skills are presented in Appendix B.

Keys to Best Practice: Ask your students to maintain learning logs and journals that assess their learning and responses to your instruction (Carr, 2002; Lenz, Graner, & Adams, 2003; Salend, 2008).

Learning Logs and Journals

You can assess your students' learning and responses to your instruction by asking them to maintain learning logs or learning journals (Carr, 2002). Thus, following a specific learning activity, your students can write entries in their logs related to the things they learned, the strategies they used to learn, the things they still need to learn, and the additional assistance they would like to receive (Lenz et al., 2003). For example, you can ask students to periodically write about

- what they learned,
- how they learned it,
- what they do not understand, and
- why they are confused and the help they need.

You can then review individual students' logs to assess their learning and make any needed adjustments in your teaching to help those students who have not yet demonstrated mastery of the specific content you have been teaching. Your students can use their learning logs and journals to provide you with information related to their attitudes toward learning and the different content areas, the extent to which lessons relate to their lives, and their suggestions about things they would like to learn. They also can use their learning logs to reflect on their learning progress over time. For example, your students can reflect on their writing skills by responding to the following questions (which can easily be modified to assess reading, mathematics, spelling, science, and social studies):

- What are some things you do well when you write?
- What are some parts of writing that cause you difficulty?
- In what ways is your writing improving?
- What areas of your writing would you like to improve?
- What strategies can help you learn how to improve your writing?

You can adjust the learning log process to accommodate the varied abilities of your students. If some of your students have difficulty writing, they can dictate their responses using a digital recorder, or they can respond to sentence completion prompts (e.g., *I learned . . . ; I don't understand . . . ; You can help me understand by . . .*).

Technology can be used to make it easier for you and your students to use learning logs. Students can maintain a self-assessment learning word-processing file or a blog that contains periodic entries related to their performance on classroom instructional activities (Davis & McGrail, 2009). You can then use technology to easily access your students' learning logs and provide them with appropriate instructional feedback based on their entries. Technology-based learning logs also can facilitate the sharing of learning logs with your students' families.

Keys to Best Practice: Survey and interview your students to understand their perceptions of their learning and school performance (Layton & Lock, 2008; Overton, 2009; Salend, 2008).

Student Surveys and Interviews

You can obtain important information from your students by surveying and interviewing them (Layton & Lock, 2008; Overton, 2009). Surveys and interviews can help you understand your students' perceptions of their learning and school performance, including their educational strengths and challenges, their progress in learning, their attitudes toward school, and the best ways they learn (Salend, 2008). You can survey or interview students at different times during the school year and use the results to note changes in their responses and to personalize your teaching. Sample questions that can be used as part of a student interview are presented in Figure 5.4.

When using surveys and interviews, consider these suggestions:

- Phrase questions so they are easy for your students to understand.
- Where possible, state questions using positive terms. For example, you can ask your students about their challenges rather than about the problems they are having.
- Begin by asking questions that address your students' strengths.
- Ask only educationally relevant questions and avoid questions that are controversial or may make students feel uncomfortable.
- Be culturally sensitive.
- Follow up by asking students to provide specific examples related to their comments.

Figure 5.4   Sample Student Interview Questions

Student Interview Questions

- How do you feel about school this year?
- What do you like about school?
- What do you dislike about school?
- What are your greatest strengths and talents in school? What do you do well in school?
- In what areas do you think you need to improve at school?
- How would you describe yourself?
- What are your successes?
- What are your dreams for the future?
- What things would you like to learn in school?
- In what ways do you learn best?
- How would you describe your behavior in school?
- How do you get along with other students in your class and in school?
- What things could your teacher(s) do to help you learn or be more successful in school?
- Are you completing your class work, homework, and assigned projects? If not, why not?
- How would you describe your study skills?
- In what school clubs or activities do you participate? If none, why not?
- What do you like to do after school? What are your hobbies?

Multimedia and software programs can be used to assess your students' interests and preferences in terms of learning, reinforcement, and careers, as well as their self-awareness. For example, *StrategyTools,* a software package that includes a range of template tools for use by you, your students, and their families, contains an online self-awareness survey and monitoring card that students can complete to assess their skills (Mitchem et al., 2007). You also can use a range of resources to create your own technology-based learning and reinforcement preference and self-awareness assessment surveys (see Appendix B and the resources for creating surveys and administering them via technology that are presented in Appendix A).

Keys to Best Practice: Use a range of classroom assessments to implement performance assessment (Overton, 2009; Spinelli, 2006).

HOW CAN I USE CLASSROOM ASSESSMENTS TO IMPLEMENT PERFORMANCE ASSESSMENT?

Performance Assessment

An excellent way to measure the impact of your classroom instruction on your students' learning is *performance assessment,* which is sometimes referred to as *authentic assessment.* Because performance assessment involves students working on meaningful, complex, relevant, open-ended instructional activities to create authentic products that relate to your curriculum, it is an excellent way to assess your students' ability to problem solve and to think critically (Spinelli, 2006). Often performance assessment involves students showing the knowledge and skills they have learned by completing assignments such as the following:

- Demonstrations and presentations
- Written products
- Cooperative learning group products
- Role plays and simulations
- Experiments
- Technology-based projects

These learning products can then be graded and aligned to curriculum learning standards and students' IEPs as a culminating authentic activity to assess student mastery of specific content, topics, concepts, and skills taught, and to communicate information about student performance to others. For example, your students' mastery of content related to an instructional unit on the human body can be assessed by having them create a replica of the human body and then showcase and explain it to others.

Keys to Best Practice: Use instructional rubrics to evaluate and reflect on student work and your instruction, and to guide your students in completing their performance assessment projects (Andrade, 2008; Stanford & Reeves, 2005; Whittaker, Salend, & Duhaney, 2001).

Instructional Rubrics

The educational skills that your students demonstrate when completing performance assessment projects can be evaluated by using *instructional rubrics,* which specify the criteria associated with different levels of proficiency for evaluating student performance (Andrade, 2008; Stanford & Reeves, 2005). The instructional rubric developed by Ms. Leon and her students is presented in Figure 5.5. While instructional rubrics can help you evaluate and reflect on student work and your instruction, and identify the skills mastered and not mastered by your students, they also can guide your students in completing performance assessment projects.

There are two types of instructional rubrics: holistic and analytic. *Holistic rubrics* involve you rating the quality of the entire assignment and are typically used for comprehensive performance assessment tasks that are related to district, state, or national standards. *Analytic rubrics,* such as the one Ms. Leon and her students created, allow you to rate the quality of different aspects of your students' learning products and are typically used to provide feedback to students on their performance.

The use of instructional rubrics has several benefits for you and your students. They can help you clarify and communicate your expectations, which can make your feedback and grading more consistent and objective. This aids your students in understanding your expectations for them and assists them in monitoring and assessing their learning and assignments.

Instructional rubrics are most likely to have these benefits when you develop them with your students using the following suggestions:

Step 1: Determine whether to use instructional rubrics to assess student learning. Identify the standards and learning goals the assignment addresses, consider the different ways to measure student mastery, and determine if the use of an instructional rubric is the best format for evaluating the performance-based assessment task and student learning.

Figure 5.5 Ms. Leon's Class's Instructional Rubric

Level of Performance Category	Beginning 1	Developing 2	Accomplished 3	Exemplary 4
Content	The purpose of the site is not stated and is focused on only one aspect of the culture 1	The purpose of the site is unclear and is focused on only one aspect of the culture 2	The purpose of the site is clear and is focused on two aspects of the culture 3	The purpose of the site is very clear and focused on more than two aspects of the culture 4
	Details, examples, illustrations, and images are missing 1	Details, examples, illustrations, and images are limited 2	Details, examples, illustrations, and images help others understand the information 3	Details, examples, illustrations, and images are very helpful to others in understanding the information 4
	Two or fewer sources of information have been discussed and referenced 1	Two to three sources of information have been discussed and referenced 2	Four or five different sources of information are discussed and referenced 3	Six or more different sources of information have been discussed and referenced 4
	The site has three or fewer content pages and no author's page 1	The site has only four content pages or no author's page 2	The site has five content pages and an author's page 3	The site has more than five content pages and an author's page 4
	Many statements and images are factually incorrect and contain stereotypes 1	Some statements and images are factually incorrect and contain stereotypes 2	Most statements and images are factually correct and free of stereotypes 3	All statements and images are factually correct and free of stereotypes 4
Design	The site is missing a title page, table of contents, and navigation buttons 1	The site is missing a title page, table of contents, or navigation buttons 2	The site has a title page, table of contents, and navigation buttons 3	The site has an innovative title page, table of contents, and is easy to navigate 4

	The visual aspects of the text and images such as line, color, value, shape, and texture are unappealing and inappropriate 1	The visual aspects of the text and images such as line, color, value, shape, and texture are either unappealing or inappropriate 2	The visual aspects of the text and images such as line, color, value, shape, and texture are appealing and appropriate 3	The visual aspects of the text and images such as line, color, value, shape, and texture are appealing and imaginative 4
Indicator →	(The layout of the text and images is confusing to the viewer) 1	The layout of the text and images is sometimes confusing to the viewer 2	The layout of the text and images is clear to the viewer 3	The layout of the text and images is clear and helpful to the viewer 4
	The site is accessible to few persons with visual or auditory disabilities 1	The site is accessible to some persons with visual or auditory disabilities 2	The site is accessible to most persons with visual or auditory disabilities 3	The site is accessible and inviting to persons with visual or auditory disabilities facts 4
Literacy Skills	The meaning of much of the text is unclear to the reader 1	The meaning of some of the text is unclear to the reader 2	The meaning of most of the text is clear to the reader 3	The meaning of all of the text is very clear to the reader 4
	The site has few new or interesting facts 1	The site has some new or interesting facts 2	The site has several new and interesting facts 3	The site has many new and interesting facts 4
	All ideas are not logically connected 1	Many ideas are not logically connected 2	Many ideas are logically connected 3	All ideas are logically connected 4
	There are many punctuation, grammar, and spelling errors 1	There are some punctuation, grammar, or spelling errors 2	There are few punctuation, grammar, or spelling errors 3	There are no punctuation, grammar, or spelling errors 4

Step 2: Examine examples of the assignment to identify important features and relevant categories. Examine examples of the assignment completed by your students in the past and identify the important features that make the assignments excellent, good, mediocre, and inadequate. Use these important features to determine the relevant categories that the instructional rubric will address. For example, the relevant categories identified by Ms. Leon and her students were content, design, and literacy skills.

Step 3: Determine the levels of performance. Create an age-appropriate scale reflecting the instructional rubric's three or four levels of performance. For example, the performance levels for Ms. Leon's instructional rubric were Beginning (1), Developing (2), Accomplished (3), and Exemplary (4). Determine whether to attach points (e.g., 1, 2, 3, 4) to each level and to weight different categories based on their importance.

Consider how to word the different levels of performance. Here are some examples of wordings that other teachers have used:

- No; no, but; yes, but; yes
- Below expectations; acceptable; proficient; excellent
- Novice; apprentice; proficient; distinguished

You can ask your students to help name the performance levels. Thus "awesome" may replace "excellent."

Step 4: Compose a set of indicators that guide you and your students in using the instructional rubric. Write *indicators*, which are brief statements that clearly present the specific features related to your instructional rubric's identified categories and different performance levels. Your indicators can

- be number-based (three or more, at least two, fewer than three, many, some, few, none),
- be time-based (all of the time, most of the time, some of the time), or
- focus on descriptive aspects (clearly established, established, unclear).

Once you compose your set of indicators, examine them to delete irrelevant ones, combine those that overlap, and add important ones that are missing.

Step 5: Make sure the instructional rubric is positive, understandable, unbiased, and doesn't stifle your students' creativity. Review your instructional rubric in terms of the following:

- Is it stated in positive terms?
- Is it understandable to students?
- Is it unbiased?
- Does it stifle creativity?

Step 6: Teach and encourage students to use the instructional rubric. Teach and encourage your students to use the instructional rubric by

- explaining it to them,
- providing models and examples of each aspect of the instructional rubric,
- asking them to use it with samples of assignments of varying quality,
- prompting them to use it when working on their assignments, and
- scheduling conferences with them to discuss their use of it.

Step 7: Evaluate students' assignments using the instructional rubric and revise the rubric accordingly. Use the instructional rubric to assess your students' work. Reflect on the impact of the rubric on your students' learning and grades and your teaching, and revise it based on your reflections (Whittaker et al., 2001).

Technology can assist you in developing and sharing your instructional rubrics. Appendix B includes Web sites you can use to create and post your own rubrics or to view and edit a bank of rubric projects developed by other professionals. Once developed and explained to your students, instructional rubrics can be posted online so that you and your students and their families can access them at their convenience.

Keys to Best Practice: Use portfolio assessment to examine student learning and to evaluate and guide your instruction (Cohen & Spenciner, 2007; Salend, 2008; Thompson, Meadan, Fansler, Alber, & Balogh, 2007).

Portfolio Assessment

Portfolio assessment is an integral part of performance assessment. Portfolio assessment involves you and your students and their families collaborating to record collections of student work over time and reflecting on these authentic items to determine what they show about student learning and your instructional program (Cohen & Spenciner, 2007; Thompson et al., 2007). Portfolios can be related to specific skills and instruction in one content area (e.g., a literacy portfolio focusing on reading and writing items) or a range of content areas (e.g., a generic portfolio displaying student work in reading, mathematics, science, social studies).

While you can use portfolios to document the learning progress, effort, attitudes, achievement, development, and learning styles of all of your students, they are particularly useful in complying with the assessment mandates for students with significant cognitive disabilities specified in NCLB and IDEIA. Thus, instead of taking high-stakes grade-level tests based on statewide learning standards, your students with significant cognitive disabilities can complete alternative assessments aligned to *alternate achievement standards* that are not as complex as grade level achievement standards (Towles-Reeves, Kleinert, & Muhomba, 2009). These modified assessments are designed for students, like Ronald, who

- take a general education class for reasons other than mastery of the general education curriculum,
- require extensive instructional modifications, and
- are not able to participate in high-stakes testing even with testing accommodations.

In many states, modified assessments involve the use of portfolios to compare student work over time and to link student learning products to statewide standards (Perner, 2007). These portfolios often take the form of digital portfolios, which contain video and audio recordings of students performing various activities related to alternate achievement standards. For example, Mr. Shaw and Ronald used a range of technologies to create a digital portfolio that included Ronald demonstrating a variety of skills aligned to statewide learning standards, as well as Ronald's digital story about his career and transitional goals.

Digital cameras, digital and audio recorders, and scanners as well as the other technologies described in this chapter can be used to record students performing academic and social activities and portfolio items (Thompson et al., 2007). A range of digital portfolio software is available to guide you and your students and colleagues in creating digital portfolios (see Appendix B). These programs offer ways to

- scan audio and digital files of student work;
- enter sound and video clips of observations and students engaged in a range of learning activities;
- import external files containing student work from other programs (e.g., word processing, presentation software, and Web page and site construction programs);
- organize portfolios by subject, theme, project, date, and title;
- link portfolio items to national, statewide, and districtwide standards, instructional rubrics, and individualized lesson plans; and
- facilitate the ease with which portfolios can be shared with others (Glor-Sheib & Telthorster, 2006).

You and your students can use the following guidelines to create portfolios (Salend, 2008).

Step 1: Establish the goals of the portfolio. You and your students establish individualized goals for their portfolio that are directly related to your curriculum. For students with special needs, portfolio goals can be aligned to IEPs, alternate learning standards, and other specific outcomes that you have to guide their learning.

Step 2: Select a portfolio type that matches the goals of the portfolio. There are several different types of portfolios. The portfolio type selected should match the portfolio goals established in Step 1. The different types of portfolios are as follows:

- *Showcase portfolios,* which present the best work done by your students
- *Cumulative portfolios,* which document changes in your students' learning over time
- *Goal-based portfolios,* which contain items that are linked to specific goals established for individual students, such as IEP goals
- *Process portfolios,* which focus on the learning styles and strategies your students use to learn

Step 3: Choose classroom learning products that address the portfolio's goals. You and your students can work collaboratively to choose the classroom learning products to be included in their portfolios. You can involve students' families in the selection process. In selecting items to be part of a portfolio consider the following questions:

- What classroom products should be included in the portfolio that show the student has made progress learning?
- What classroom learning products should be included in the portfolio that show the processes and learning strategies the student employs?

You can help involve students in the selection process by providing them with examples and a menu of possible portfolio items. You can guide them in identifying their favorite and most difficult items; the items that show their learning progress, problem-solving skills, and creativity; and the items that show their mastery of specific skills related to the goals of the portfolio.

Step 4: Collect and organize portfolio items. Items selected for inclusion in portfolios are collected digitally or placed in individualized file folders, binders, or boxes with dividers. Selected items can then be organized based on the portfolio goals or by chronological order (e.g., early, intermediate, later works), academic or content area subjects, and student interests. Students can personalize their portfolios in age-appropriate ways using photographs, pictures, logos, and other symbols that have meaning to them.

Step 5: Create caption statements to note the significance of items included in the portfolios. For each portfolio item, you and your students should create *caption statements*, short written descriptions that identify the item and explain the context in which it was produced and why it was included in the portfolio. A sample caption statement is presented in Figure 5.6.

Step 6: Foster teacher and student reflection. Caption statements include reflections by you and your students regarding what the item shows about student learning (see Figure 5.6). You can examine the item and reflect on what it shows about your students' learning as well as the process and strategies your students used to learn and complete the assignment.

You can take several actions to foster student reflection. You can ask your students to respond to questions such as the following:

1. What was the assignment? (Describe the assignment.)

2. What things did I do well on this assignment?

3. What things did I learn from working on this assignment?

4. What strategies and techniques did I use to work on the assignment?

5. How could I improve this assignment?

Figure 5.6   Sample Portfolio Caption Statement

Item Description: Betty was asked to look through past assignments and to pick pieces of work that represented something new and exciting that she had learned this year. Betty said she chose Item A because it was a topic she really enjoyed. Item A is a journal entry in which Betty was required to write an explanation and provide two examples of how to use the Pythagorean Theorem for a friend who was absent.

Teacher Reflection: One of the things that I really stress to my students is to "think outside of the box." I want the students to be able to take the content that is learned in class and apply the information in their everyday lives. I think that Betty did an excellent job of developing two real-life examples to present in her journal.

Betty's explanations show that she really understands and has a good grasp of the concepts. She labeled the sides of the triangles and showed all the work in completing each step of the process. She began solving the problems by recalling and stating the formula for Pythagorean's Theorem and then showed each step as she worked on the problem.

Student Reflection: I chose this journal entry for my portfolio because I spent a lot of time on it. I liked the activities that we did when we first learned about right triangles and Pythagoras, which has helped me to understand the theorem. Solving for the lengths of the legs and hypotenuse was challenging at first, but then I got the hang of it and it was really easy. Instead of just showing examples of how to find the lengths of sides, I tried to think of real-life examples so that the friend that I was explaining it to would really understand the topic.

You also can foster your students' reflection by having them write or dictate letters to their portfolio

- comparing items over time (e.g., *What changes have you noticed in your reading over time?*);
- discussing the reasons why a specific item was included in their portfolio; and
- identifying patterns among items (e.g., *What patterns have you noticed in your writing?*).

Since some of your students may experience difficulty reflecting, peer or adult scribes or audio and video recordings can be employed to facilitate their participation in the self-reflection process. You also can provide them with caption statement prompts such as the ones presented in Figure 5.7.

Figure 5.7   Sample Caption Statement Prompts

Improvements

This work shows my improvement in _____. I used to _____, but now I _____.

Pride

I am proud of this assignment because _____. In this assignment, notice how I _____.

Special Efforts

This assignment shows something that is difficult for me. As you can see, I have made a special effort to ___.

IEP Goals

This assignment shows my progress on _____. I have learned to _____. I will continue to _____.

Academic Areas

In [academic area], I have been working on _____. My goal is to _____.

Thematic Units

I have been working on learning about the theme of _____. As part of this unit, I chose the following items: _____. These items show that I _____.

Projects

I have been working on a project on _____. I learned _____. The project shows I can _____.

Challenges

This work shows the challenges I have with _____.

Strategy Use

I used the following method to work on this item: _____.

The steps I used to learn this were: _____.

Source: Adapted from Countryman & Schroeder (1996).

Step 7: Review portfolios to assess student learning and the instructional program. Portfolios should be reviewed periodically by you and your students and their families to discuss the impact of the instructional program on student learning. At these meetings, your students can introduce their portfolios to others by

- identifying the goals and purpose of their portfolios,
- explaining how their portfolios are organized and have been individualized,
- giving an overview of the contents and special items in their portfolios,
- reviewing the criteria for evaluating their portfolios and individual items, and
- outlining what the portfolios show regarding their school performance.

After the introduction, portfolios can be examined to assess the student's

- educational, behavioral, language, and social-emotional performance and skills;
- strengths and challenges; and
- learning styles, attitudes, motivation, interests, and use of learning strategies.

The portfolio also should be examined to determine ways to enhance the student's educational program.

Keys to Best Practice: Use a range of technology-based projects to implement performance assessment (King-Sears & Evmenova, 2007; Knobel & Wilber, 2009; November, 2008).

HOW CAN I USE TECHNOLOGY TO IMPLEMENT PERFORMANCE ASSESSMENT?

Technology-Based Performance Assessment

The use of technology is an excellent way to implement performance assessment. In addition to showcasing your students' academic skills, technology-based performance assessment can promote your students' technology skills (King-Sears & Evmenova, 2007).

Keys to Best Practice: Consider whether the use of technology is an appropriate way to assess classroom instruction, tasks, and skills (Salend, 2008).

Before using technology-based performance assessments, you should consider whether use of technology facilitates the teaching, learning, and assessment processes without altering the classroom instruction, tasks, and skills that are being taught and assessed. For example, whereas writing a blog might be an appropriate activity for assessing a range of narrative writing skills, creating a digital PowerPoint presentation may not be the best way to assess students' narrative writing.

Keys to Best Practice: Teach your students how to be good digital citizens who use technology in a safe, responsible, and appropriate manner (Badke, 2009; Moore, Howard & Davies, 2009; Mustacchi, 2009; November, 2008).

Prior to using technology-based classroom assessments, you need to provide your students with instruction to help them learn how to be good digital citizens who use technology in a safe, responsible, and appropriate manner (Badke, 2009; Mustacchi, 2009; November, 2008). You can establish and teach rules, etiquette, and common sense for using the Internet and protecting their privacy. As part of this instruction, you need to teach your students to avoid inappropriate Web sites and to refrain from posting or giving out personal information and pictures. They should be taught about viruses and spam and how to avoid them. Your students should learn how to conduct searches and interact with others as well as what constitutes and how to avoid cyberbullying and plagiarism (see Moore et al., [2009] and Mustacchi [2009] for suggestions and strategies for teaching your students about cyberbullying and plagiarism). You can use the guidelines presented in Figure 5.8 to teach your students how to evaluate Web sites and Web-based information. It is important for you to monitor your students' use of technology during instruction to make sure students are using it appropriately. When using technology-based classroom assessments with your students with special needs, you need to provide them with access to the assistive technology they require to participate in these assessment activities (see Chapter 3).

Keys to Best Practice: Exercise caution and take appropriate and effective safeguards when sharing student work with others via technology (November, 2008).

Figure 5.8   Guidelines for Evaluating Web Sites and Web-Based Information

- Who produced the site? When and why did they produce it?
- Does the title of the site reflect the content presented?
- Is contact information for the site available?
- Is the site produced by a credible individual, organization, or group?
- What are the goals and purposes of the site?
- Does the site have a specific agenda and any biases?
- Is the information provided current, accurate, helpful, and detailed?
- Is the information presented free of opinions, errors, emotional appeals, and biases?
- Are useful supporting visuals provided?
- Who provided the information for the site?
- Are the credentials of the author(s) of the information provided? Appropriate?
- Are sources of the information provided, relevant, and cited correctly?
- Are relevant links to other sites provided? Are these links active, up-to-date, appropriate, and useful?
- Is the site frequently updated?
- When was the site last updated?

Technologies such as presentation software, blogs, digital videos, podcasts, and wikis have the advantage of making student work more authentic because it can be shared with and used by others easily (November, 2008). However, it is critical that you exercise caution and take safeguards when sharing students' work with others. Therefore prior to posting student work online, you should make sure that the digital environment is safe and secure. You can do this by

- obtaining permission from students, their families, and your school district to post student work,
- deleting confidential and personally identifying information from students' work,
- requiring your students to use pseudonyms and numbers instead of their real names,
- blocking out visuals of students,
- vetting the content and visuals to make sure they are appropriate for viewing by others,
- using password protection to control who can post and view student work, and
- limiting access so that only your students and their families can view their work (November, 2008).

Several technologies appear to be particularly useful for students to present the products of their learning. These technologies, which are discussed in the following sections, include using presentation software, creating online and digital learning products such as Web pages and sites, blogs, podcasts, and digital movies or stories, engaging in computer simulations and virtual learning experiences, completing WebQuests and Tracks, and using wikis.

Keys to Best Practice: Teach your students to use presentation software to present the outcomes of their learning (Doyle & Giangreco, 2009; Schleibaum, 2007; Skouge, Kelly, Roberts, Leake, & Stodden, 2007).

Using Presentation Software

Presentation software such as PowerPoint, Keynote, and Impress (see Appendix B) can be used by your students to present the outcomes of their learning to others (Doyle & Giangreco, 2009; Skouge et al., 2007). For example, your students can use such software to give a presentation explaining important aspects of the solar system to others. In addition to highlighting the key points and vocabulary related to the topic, these presentations can include the use of color, animation, audio, videos, visuals, and links to related Web sites. You can help your students improve the quality of their presentations by teaching them to (a) access and use appropriate and high quality visuals; (b) limit the text presented on each slide so that each slide contains six or fewer words per line and no more than six lines; (c) focus the slides on big ideas and key points; (d) integrate relevant short audio and video segments; (e) refrain from overusing animation features; and (f) select contrasting background and text colors (Doyle & Giangreco, 2009). The presentation software resources presented in Appendix B can guide your students in working collaboratively and adding video, visuals, television-style backgrounds, audio, animation, and hyperlinks. Your students can use various software programs and Web sites, such as Slideshare (www.slideshare.net) and Bookr (www .pimpampum.net/bookr), to create online slideshows and share them with others.

Your students can use presentation software to prepare a digital task analysis or social story that demonstrates their ability to perform specific academic, social, behavioral, transitional, and functional skills (Schleibaum, 2007). This involves taking digital images (video or pictures) of each step in a task analysis or social story and converting the digital images into presentation software slides that include brief written and oral descriptions of each step in the task analysis or each event in the social story.

Keys to Best Practice: Teach your students to create Web pages or sites to demonstrate and share their learning with others (March, 2006; Richardson, 2006; Salend, 2008).

Creating Web Pages and Sites

You can teach your students to create Web pages or sites to demonstrate and share their learning with others (March, 2006; Richardson, 2006). As Ms. Leon did, your students can post their work on your class's Web page or create Web pages or sites presenting their assignments and then receive and respond to comments and questions from others about their postings. While most Internet service providers offer Web page or site creation software, resources that offer easy-to-use assistance and services for creating and maintaining Web pages and sites are presented in Appendix B.

Keys to Best Practice: Teach your students to compose Web logs (blogs) to present the outcomes of their learning (Davis & McGrail, 2009; Knobel & Wilber, 2009; March, 2006; Richardson, 2006; Schweder & Wissick, 2007).

Composing Web Logs (Blogs)

Your students' work can take the form of *Web logs (blogs),* online commentaries that can be updated regularly by you and your students to present their assignments and to share their knowledge of a specific topic and across the curriculum (Davis & McGrail, 2009; Schweder & Wissick, 2007). In addition to text, blogs can contain pictorials and video clips (these blogs are referred to as vlogs), audio files such as music or narration, and links to other related Web sites. Blogs are good ways to extend classroom discussions or question-and-answer sessions beyond the confines of classrooms. Individuals and groups of students can maintain blogs to share information about things they have learned, to comment on learning experiences and events, and to interact with others (Knobel & Wilber, 2009). Resources to assist you and your students in creating and maintaining blogs are presented in Appendix B.

Keys to Best Practice: Teach your students to produce podcasts to present the outcomes of their learning (Williams, 2007).

Producing Podcasts

Your students also can display their learning by producing podcasts (Williams, 2007). Although podcasts originally were audio recordings of events or blogs, today's podcasts frequently integrate audio and video to present information about a specific topic or to record a specific activity. For example, you and your students can create podcasts of them engaged in such classroom activities as giving book reports and reviews, performing experiments and class plays, and discussing topics. When creating podcasts to share with others, it is helpful to include markers, which allow others to easily locate or access specific parts of the podcast. Resources related to creating and posting podcasts and using presentation capture software programs to record and convert classroom activities into podcasts that have synchronized audio and visual images are presented in Appendix B.

Keys to Best Practice: Teach your students to create digital videos and stories to showcase the outcomes of their learning and to communicate relevant information about themselves (Kaylor, 2008; Rao, Dowrick, Yuen, & Boisvert, 2009; Skouge et al., 2007; Sprankle, 2008; Thompson et al., 2007).

Creating Digital Videos and Stories

Your students can learn how to produce digital videos and stories to showcase the outcomes of their learning and communicate relevant information about themselves (Rao et al., 2009). Your students can use digital cameras and camcorders and audio recorders to record video and audio material and then use the software programs presented in Appendix B to create digital videos or stories presenting role-plays, documentaries, narratives, news reports, essays, poems, book reports, interviews, and skill demonstrations (Sprankle, 2008). These programs allow your students to record narrations to describe learning products, processes, and outcomes and to integrate music and artwork. For example, your students can make digital videos showcasing their best learning experiences throughout the school year that include their narration of what they have learned and how they learned it.

Once developed, these digital videos can be shared with others, including students' families, via e-mail and posting them on your class's Web site. In addition, Web sites such as TeacherTube (www.teachertube.com) and SchoolTube (www.schooltube.com) allow you to share your classroom-appropriate videos with others. Your students can showcase and receive feedback on their work or comment on the work of others via use of Ed.VoiceThread.com (www.voicethread .com), a secure collaborative network for K–12 students and educators that allows students to provide or receive comments on digital images, videos, documents, and presentations.

Digital storytelling is a particularly good format for your students to present their skills and share information about themselves with others (Kaylor, 2008; Skouge et al., 2007). For example, Ronald worked with Mr. Shaw to create a digital story of his life, career preferences, and transition goals that contained pictures and video paired with text- and audio-based narratives of Ronald working with classmates, interacting with family and friends, and participating in various extracurricular community activities. Resources providing additional information about making digital stories and videos and posting them online are listed in Appendix B.

Keys to Best Practice: Use computer simulations and virtual learning experiences to assess your students' responses to a range of learning situations and their academic, critical thinking, social, and metacognitive skills (Cote, 2007; Cummings, 2007; Gee & Levine, 2009; Sayeski, 2008; Smedley & Higgins, 2005).

Engaging in Computer Simulations and Virtual Learning Experiences

Engaging your students in computer simulations and virtual learning experiences can be used to assess their responses to a range of learning situations and their academic, critical thinking, social, and metacognitive skills (Cote, 2007; Cummings, 2007). Via problem-solving, simulation, and virtual learning software programs and Web sites, your student responses to authentic learning experiences and multidimensional dilemmas and situations across the curriculum can be assessed (Gee & Levine, 2009; Sayeski, 2008; Smedley & Higgins, 2005). For example, you can use the following simulations and virtual learning experiences to foster and assess your students' mastery of content across the curriculum:

- *The Technology-Based Assessment Project* (nces.ed.gov/nationsreportcard/studies/tbaproject.asp) has developed computer-based search and simulation activities to assess students' physical science knowledge, as well as their problem-solving and technology skills.
- *River City Project* (http://muve.gse.harvard.edu/muvees2003/) includes interactive and collaborative group computer simulations to teach and assess content linked to the National Science Education Standards and the National Education Technology Standards.
- *Immune Attack* (www.fas.org/immuneattack) provides a simulation activity related to the human immune system developed by the Federation of American Sciences that uses a 3-D video game format with an assessment feature that requires students to answer a series of questions before proceeding to the next level of the simulation.
- *The Virtual History Museum* (vhm.msu.edu/site/default.php) offers students access to digital artifacts and primary source documents that they can use to complete a variety of products that assess their learning of history (Okolo, Englert, Bouck, & Heutsche, 2007).
- *Interactive Mathematics on the Internet* (wims.unice.fr/wims/en_home.html) provides interactive mathematics-based online activities for assessing student learning.
- *Explore Learning* (www.explorelearning.com) offers opportunities for students to engage in online interactive simulations related to math and science.
- *The Virtual Courseware Project* (www.sciencecourseware.org) provides access to interactive, online simulations that are aligned to National Science Education Learning Standards.

Additional resources to help you and your students design and engage in computer simulations and virtual learning experiences across the curriculum are presented in Appendix B. When using these virtual learning and assessment techniques, it is important to make sure that your students can generalize and apply these skills in real settings and learning environments.

Completing WebQuests and Tracks

Teachers like Ms. Leon are finding that *WebQuests* and *Tracks* are excellent online activities for fostering and assessing students. A *WebQuest* is an inquiry-oriented, cooperatively structured group activity in which some or all of the information presented to learners comes from resources on the Internet (Skylar et al., 2007). WebQuests can be structured in a variety of ways including Internet hunts, puzzles, projects, and study guides. Like other projects produced by collaborative learning groups, you can evaluate WebQuests based on the groups' mastery of subject matter as well as on their ability to work together. Each group member's mastery of the content presented in the WebQuest can be assessed via individualized quizzes or probes.

A *Track* is an online lesson that involves students engaging in a variety of instructional activities by visiting a series of teacher-specified Web sites. You can then assess your students' learning by examining their learning products or by having them complete an online quiz of material presented via the Track. Web sites providing guidelines and resources to assist you in creating WebQuests and Tracks and accessing a database of WebQuests and Tracks developed by other educators are presented in Appendix B.

Using Wikis

Your students also can display their learning by using *wikis,* which are online Web pages addressing a range of topics, updated and edited by visitors to the site (March, 2006). Thus, your students can share what they know about a specific topic by creating a new wiki or editing an existing wiki (Knobel & Wilber, 2009; Schweder & Wissick, 2009). Your students can receive feedback on their wiki entries by periodically viewing the wiki to see the comments and changes made by others. For example, your students can use Wikipedia (www.wikipedia.org), a collaborative encyclopedia that allows users to obtain and provide information and links on a range of different topics. When using wikis, it is essential that you and your students verify the accuracy of the information they post and carefully evaluate the information posted by others (see Figure 5.8; Badke, 2009). Other resources to assist you in identifying and starting wikis are presented in Appendix B.

SUMMARY

This chapter provided best practices you can use to implement a range of classroom assessments. You can use the reflectlist (see Figure 5.9) to review the main points presented in this chapter and to examine the extent to which you are applying best

Figure 5.9   Reflectlist for Using Classroom Assessments

Reflect on your use of classroom assessments by rating the extent to which you are applying the following keys to best practices.

Keys to Best Practice	Often	Sometimes	Rarely	Never
I use a range of classroom assessments to monitor the learning progress of my students.	☐	☐	☐	☐
I use curriculum-based measurement to assess my students' learning progress.	☐	☐	☐	☐
I use active responding systems to conduct real-time assessments of my students' learning and to check their understanding of the content and skills I have taught.	☐	☐	☐	☐
I use observations to assess my students' academic performance and classroom-related behaviors.	☐	☐	☐	☐
I use academic games and technology-based educational games to assess my students' learning.	☐	☐	☐	☐
I ask my students to maintain learning logs and journals that assess their learning and responses to instruction.	☐	☐	☐	☐
I survey and interview my students to understand their perceptions of their learning and school performance.	☐	☐	☐	☐
I use a range of classroom assessments to implement performance assessment.	☐	☐	☐	☐
I use instructional rubrics to evaluate and reflect on student work and my instruction, and to guide my students in completing their performance assessment projects.	☐	☐	☐	☐
I use portfolio assessment to examine student learning and to evaluate and guide my instruction.	☐	☐	☐	☐
I use a range of technology-based projects to implement performance assessment.	☐	☐	☐	☐
I consider whether the use of technology is an appropriate way to assess classroom instruction, tasks, and skills.	☐	☐	☐	☐

Figure 5.9   Reflectlist for Using Classroom Assessments

Keys to Best Practice	Often	Sometimes	Rarely	Never
I teach my students how to be good digital citizens who use technology in a safe, responsible, and appropriate manner.	☐	☐	☐	☐
I exercise caution and take appropriate and effective safeguards when sharing student work with others via technology.	☐	☐	☐	☐
My students use presentation software to present the outcomes of their learning.	☐	☐	☐	☐
My students create Web pages and sites to demonstrate and share their learning with others.	☐	☐	☐	☐
My students compose Web logs (blogs) to present the outcomes of their learning.	☐	☐	☐	☐
My students produce podcasts to present the outcomes of their learning.	☐	☐	☐	☐
My students create digital videos and stories to showcase the outcomes of their learning and to communicate relevant information about themselves.	☐	☐	☐	☐
I use computer simulations and virtual learning experiences to assess my students' responses to a range of learning situations and their academic, critical thinking, social, and metacognitive skills.	☐	☐	☐	☐
I use WebQuests and Tracks to foster and assess my students' learning.	☐	☐	☐	☐
My students display their learning by using wikis.	☐	☐	☐	☐

- How would you rate your use of classroom assessments?
- What aspects are your strengths?
- In what areas do you need to improve?
- What steps can you take to improve your use of classroom assessments?

practices to implement classroom assessments. These assessments can be used to supplement the testing practices we discussed in earlier chapters to monitor your students' learning progress and inform your instructional decision making so that you can make appropriate adjustments to improve your teaching for all of your students.

Appendix A

Test Creation and Administration Resource Web Sites

Technology-Based Gaming Resources

Funbrain (www.funbrain.com)

Brainpop (www.brainpop.com)

Everyday Math Games (www.emgames.com)

Interactive Whiteboards in the Classroom (www.fsdb.k12.fl.us/mc/tutorials/whiteboards.html#sites)

Homemade Powerpoint Games (it.coe.uga.edu/wwild/pptgames)

Text- and Screen-Reading Program Resources

Read and Write Gold (TextHELP) (www.readwritegold.com/index.html)

TextAssist (www.textassist.com)

TextAloud (www.nextup.com/Text Aloud)

Wynn and JAWS (www.freedomscientific.com)

ReadPlease (www.readplease.com)

EasyReader (www.yourdolphin.com/productdetail.asp?id=9)

ZoomText (www.aisquared.com/index.cfm)

Window-Eyes (www.gwmicro.com/Window-Eyes)

NaturalReader (www.naturalreaders.com)

Optical Character Reading (OCR) Systems Resources

Kurzweil-National Federation of the Blind Reader (www.knfbreader.com)

ReadingPen (www.readingpen.com)

Scan Pen (www.cpen.com)

Screen Magnification Program Resources

MAGic (www.freedomscientific.com/low-vision-help/MAGic_main.html)

ZoomText (www.aisquared.com)

Myreader2 (www.ulva.com/Online-Store/Video-Magnifiers/myreader.htm)

Assistive Listening Devices Resources

Califone (www.califone.com)

Listen Technologies Corporation (www.listentech.com)

TeachLogic (www.teachlogic.com)

Telex Communications (www.telex.com/education)

FrontRow (www.gofrontrow.com)

Audio Enhancement (www.audioenhancement.com)

Alternative Methods for Using Technology Resources

Fentek Industries (www.fentek-ind.com)

Madentec (www.madentec.com)

AccessAmerica (www.accessamericaat.com)

Access Ingenuity (www.accessingenuity.com)

Augmentative Communication Systems Resources

DynaVox Techologies (www.dynavoxtech.com)

Words+ (www.words-plus.com)

Zygo (www.zygo-usa.com)

Voice-Recognition and Activation Systems Resources

Dragon Systems Naturally Speaking (www.dragontalk.com/NATURAL.htm)

ViaVoice (www.nuance.com/viavoice/pro)

iListen (www.macspeech.com)

Talking Word Processor Resources

WriteAway (www.is-inc.com)

Write:Outloud (www.donjohnston.com/products/write_outloud/index.html)

SpeakQ (www.wordq.com/speakqenglish.html)

Word Cueing and Prediction Resources

WordQ (www.wordq.com)

Soothsayer (www.ahf-net.com/sooth.htm)

GUS! Word Prediction (www.gusinc.com/wordprediction.html)

Co:Writer (www.donjohnston.com/products/cowriter)

Electronic Dictionary and Thesaurus Resources

Wordsmyth (www.wordsmyth.net)

VoyCaBulary (www.voycabulary.com)

Visuwords (www.visuwords.com)

Visual Thesaurus (www.thinkmap.com)

Outlining and Semantic Mapping Software Resources

Inspiration and Kidspiration (www.inspiration.com)

Draft Builder (www.donjohnston.com)

Timeliner (www.tomsnyder.com)

Word Usage and Grammar Checkers Resources

WhiteSmoke (www.whitesmoke.com)

Grammar Expert Plus (www.wintertree-software.com)

StyleWriter (www.writersupercenter.com/stylewriter)

Essay Grading and Feedback Program Resources

SAGrader (www.ideaworks.com/sagrader)

My Access (www.myaccess.com/myaccess/ do/log)

WriteToLearn (www.writetolearn.net)

Criterion Online Writing Evaluation (www.ets.org)

Summary Street (www.pearsonkt.com/prodSSt.shtml)

Intellimetric (www.vantagelearning.com/school/products/intellimetric)

Online Test Preparation Resources

Practiceplanet (www.practiceplanet.com/index.php)

Study Island (www.studyisland.com)

The Online Test Page (www.saab.org/saab_org.cgi)

The Online Math Tests Home Page (mathonline.missouri.edu)

Test and Survey Creation Software Resources

TestTalker (www.freedomscientific.com/LSG/products/testtalker.asp)

Premier Test Builder (www.readingmadeez.com/education/TestBuilder.html)

LS Test Builder (www.learningstation.com/solutions/test_builder.html)

Teacher's Pet (www.aph.org/products/tp_bro.html)

Marvel Math (www.braillebookstore.com/view.php?C=Marvel+Math+ for+Windows)

ExamView's Asssesment Suite (www.fscreations.com/examview.php)

Scantron (www.scantron.com)

Pearson Educational Measuremen(www.pearsonedmeasurement.com)

Test Pilot (www.clearlearning.com)

Perceptions (www.questionmark.com/us/perception/index.htm)

Survey Monkey (www.surveymonkey.com)

Supersurvey (www.supersurvey.com)

Pollcat (www.pollcat.com)

Profiler Pro (www.profilerpro.com)

Zoomerang (www.zoomerang.com)

Online Quiz Creation and Administration Resources

Quizlab.com (www.quizlab.com)

Quizstar (quizstar.4teachers.org)

Quia (www.quia.com)

Quiz Center (school.discoveryeducation.com/quizcenter/quizcenter.html)

Moodle (docs.moodle.org/en/Features#Quiz_Module)

Technology Accessibility Resources

Web Accessibility Initiative (www.w3.org/WAI)

World Wide Web Consortium (www.w3.org/TR/WCAG20/#guidelines)

A-Prompt: Web Accessibility Verifier (aprompt.snow.utoronto.ca)

Cynthia Says (www.cynthiasays.com)

AccMonitor, AccVerify, and AccRepair (www.hisoftware.com)

Computer Accommodations Program (cap.umn.edu)

Center for Applied Special Technology (www.cast.org/index.html)

Note: The technology-based testing resources presented here are examples and should not be interpreted as an endorsement of any Web site or products.

Source: From "Using technology to create and administer accessible tests," by S. J. Salend, *Teaching Exceptional Children, 41*(3), 2009, p. 44, Copyright 2009 by the Council for Exceptional Children. Reprinted with permission.

Appendix B

Web Sites Addressing Technology-Based Classroom Assessment Strategies, Equipment, and Resources

Curriculum-Based Measurement

National Center on Student Progress Monitoring (www.studentprogress.org)

AIMS Web (www.aimsweb.com/index.php)

Curriculum-Based Measurement Warehouse (www.interventioncentral.org/htmdocs/interventions/cbmwarehouse.php)

Research Institute on Progress Monitoring (www.progressmonitoring.net)

Precision Teaching (www.precisionteachingresource.net)

Wireless Generation (www.wgen.net)

Measures of Academic Progress (www.nwea.org/assessments/map.asp)

Technology-Based Active Responding Systems

Vanderbilt Center for Teaching: Classroom Response Systems (www.vanderbilt.edu/cft/resources/teaching_resources/technology/crs.htm)

Teaching and Learning Center at University of Nevada at Las Vegas (tlc.unlv.edu/tech/clickers.htm)

Technology-Based Observational Systems

eCove (http://ecove.net)

Observer XT (www.noldus.com)

Studiocode (www.studiocodegroup.com)

The Ecobehavioral Assessment Software Systems (EBASS) (http://jgcp.ku.edu/~jgcp/products/EBASS/index.htm)

Technology-Based Educational Games

Funbrain (www.funbrain.com)

The Education Arcade (www.educationarcade.org)

Mindpoint Quizshow (http://www.einstruction.com/products/interactive_teaching/mindpoint/index.html)

Gameshow Prep (www.learningware.com)

Brainpop (www.brainpop.com)

Everyday Math Games (www.emgames.com)

Interactive Whiteboards in the Classroom (www.fsdb.k12.fl.us/rmc/tutorials/ whiteboards.html#sites)

IKnowthat.com (www.Iknowthat.com)

Write On Powerpoint Games (jc-schools.net/write/games/index.html)

Classroom Game Templates and More (www.murray.k12.ga.us/teacher/ kara%201eonard/Mini%20T's/Games/Games.htm)

Homemade Powerpoint Games (it.coe.uga.edu/wwild/pptgames)

Powerpoint Games (jc-schools.net/tutorials/PPT-games)

OLogy (www.ology.amnh.org)

Mind Reading: The Interactive Guide to Emotions (www.jkp.com/mindreading)

Preference and Self-Awareness Assessment Surveys

Jackpot Reinforcer Survey Generator (www.jimwrightonline.com/php/jackpot/ jackpot.php)

Strategy Tools (www.strategytools.org)

Survey Monkey (www.surveymonkey.com)

Supersurvey (www.supersurvey.com)

Instructional Rubrics

RubiStar (rubistar.4teachers.org/index.php)

Rubrics for Teachers (rubrics4teachers.com)

The Technology Applications Center for Educational Development (www.tcet.unt .edu/START/instruct/general/rubrics.htm)

Digital Portfolios

Grady Profile (www.aurbach.com/gp3/index.html)

Pupil Pages (www.pupilpages.com)

Portfolio Assessment Kit (www.superschoolsoftware.com/portfolios.html)

Measured Progress ProFile (www.measuredprogress.org/assessments/largescale/ special/software.html)

Presentation Software

PowerPoint (http://office.microsoft.com/en-us/powerpoint/default.aspx)

Keynote (www.apple.com/iwork/keynote)

Impress (http://presentationsoft.about.com/od/openofficeimpress/Open_Office_ Impress_Free_Presentation_Software.htm)

Ovation (www.adobe.com/products/ovation)

Impatica for PowerPoint (www.impatica.com/imp4ppt)

Preezo (www.preezo.com)

Web Page/Site Creation

TeacherWeb (www.teacherweb.com)

Eboard (www.eboard.com)

WebPlus (freeserifsoftware.com/software/WebPlus/default.asp)

Web Studio (www.webstudio.com)

Blogs

Edublogs (www.edublogs.org)

Vlog It! (www.adobe.com/products/vlogit)

Blogger (www.blogger.com)

Class Blogmeister (www.classblogmeister.com)

Word Press (www.wordpress.org)

Podcasts

Learninginhand (www.learninginhand.com/podcasting/index.html)

Education Podcast Network (www.epnweb.org/index.php?view_mode=about)

Presentation Capture Software

Premier Presentation Capture (www.readingmadeez.com/education/VCast.html)

Tegrity Campus 2.0 (www.tegrity.com)

Ech0360 (www.apreso.com)

Digital Video Software

Movie Maker (www.microsoft.com/windowsxp/downloads/updates/
moviemaker2.mspx)

Photo Story (www.microsoft.com/windowsxp/using/digitalphotography/
photostory/default.mspx)

iMovie (www.apple.com/ilife/imovie)

Premier Elements (www.adobe.com/products/premiereel)

Visual Communicator (www.adobe.com/products/visualcommunicator)

Flickr (www.Flickr.com)

ScreenCast (www.screencast.com)

MediaBlender (www.tech4learning.com/mediablender/index.html)

Pinnacle Studio (www.pinnaclesys.com/PublicSite/us/Home)

Digital Storytelling

Center for Digital Storytelling (www.storycenter.org/index1.html)

Educational Uses of Digital Storytelling (http://digitalstorytelling.coe.uh.edu)

Computer Simulations and Virtual Learning Experiences

Technology-Based Assessment Project (nces.ed.gov/nationsreportcard/studies/tbaproject.asp)

Immune Attack (www.fas.org/immuneattack)

Virtual History Museum (vhm.msu.edu/site/default.php)

FutureLab (www.simulations-plus.com/futurelab)

River City Project (http://muve.gse.harvard.edu/muvees2003/)

Try Science (www.tryscience.org)

Interactive Mathematics on the Internet (wims.unice.fr/wims/en_home.html)

Explore Learning (www.explore learning.com)

The Virtual Courseware Project (www.sciencecourseware.org)

Newbyte Educational Software (www.newbyte.com)

Alice (www.alice.org)

Epistemic Games (http://epistemicgames.org/eg/?cat=5)

Quest Atlantis (http://atlantis.crlt.indiana.edu)

WebQuests and Tracks

Webquest.Org (www.webquest.org/index.php)

Trackstar (trackstar.4teachers.org/trackstar)

Trailfire (www.trailfire.com)

Wikis

Classroom Wiki (class_room_wiki.seedwiki.com)

Peanut Butter Wiki (www.pbwiki.com/education.wiki)

WikiMatrix (www.wikimatrix.org)

Wiki.com (www.wiki.com)

Wikispaces (www.wikispaces.com)

Note: The Web sites and resources presented here are examples and should not be interpreted as an endorsement of any Web site or products.

References

Abell, M., Bauder, D., & Simmons, T. (2004). Universally designed online assessment: Implications for the future. *Information Technology and Disabilities, 10*(1). Retrieved June 1, 2007, from http://www.rit.edu/~easi/itd/itdv10n1/abell.htm

Acrey, C., Johnstone, C., & Milligan, C. (2005). Using universal design to unlock the potential for academic achievement of at-risk learners. *Teaching Exceptional Children, 38*(2), 22–31.

Albus, D., Thurlow, M., Liu, K., & Bielinski, J. (2005). Reading test performance of English language learners using an English dictionary. *The Journal of Educational Research, 98*, 245–253.

Andrade, H. (2008). Self-assessments through rubrics. *Educational Leadership, 65*(4), 60–63.

Badke, W. (2009). Stepping beyond Wikipedia. *Educational Leadership, 66*(6), 54–55.

Barber, M., & Njus, D. (2007). Clicker evolution: Seeking intelligent design. *CBE-Life Sciences Education, 6*(1), 1–8.

Barlow, C. L., & Wetherill, K. S. (2005). Technology + imagination = results. *T.H.E. Journal, 33*, 20–22, 24, 26. Retrieved May 30, 2007, from http://www.thejournal.com/articles/17431_1

Beatty, I., Gerace, W., Leonard, W., & Dufresne, R. (2006). Designing effective questions for classroom response system teaching. *American Journal of Physics, 74*(1), 31–39.

Beddow, P. A., Kettler, R. J., & Elliott, S. N. (2008). *TAMI: Test accessibility and modification inventory.* Retrieved September 22, 2008, from http://peabody.vanderbilt.edu/TAMI.xml

Bender, W. N., & Shores, C. (2007). *Response to intervention: A practical guide for teachers.* Thousand Oaks, CA: Corwin.

Bennett, D. E., Zentall, S. S., French, B. F., & Giorgetti-Borucki, K. (2006). The effects of computer administered choice on students with and without characteristics of attention-deficit/hyperactivity disorder. *Behavioral Disorders, 31*, 189–203.

Boone, R., & Higgins, K. (2007). The software-list: Evaluating educational software for use by students with disabilities. *Technology in Action, 3*(1), 1–15.

Bouck, E. C. (2006). Online assessments in the content areas: What are they good for? *Journal of Special Education Technology, 21*(2), 67–73.

Bouck, E. C., & Bouck, M. K. (2008). Does it add up? Calculators as accommodations for sixth grade students with disabilities. *Journal of Special Education Technology, 23*(2), 17–32.

Brigham Young University Counseling and Career Center. (2008). *Test-taking strategies.* Retrieved July 8, 2008 from http://ccc.byu.edu/learning/strategy.php#6

Brinckerhoff, L. C., & Banerjee, M. (2007). Misconceptions regarding accommodations on high-stakes tests: Recommendations for preparing disability documentation for test takers with learning disabilities. *Learning Disabilities Research and Practice, 22*, 246–255.

Brody, J. E. (2006, March 7). Latest in technology gives life a clearer focus. *New York Times*, p. F7.

Brookhart, S. M., & Nitko, A. J. (2008). *Assessment and grading in classrooms.* Columbus, OH: Merrill/Prentice Hall.

Byrnes, M. A. (2008). Educators' interpretations of ambiguous accommodations. *Remedial and Special Education, 29*(3), 306–315.

Capizzi, A. M., & Fuchs, L. S. (2005). Effects of curriculum-based measurement with and without diagnostic feedback on teacher planning. *Remedial and Special Education, 26*, 159–174.

Carr, S. C. (2002). Assessing learning processes: Useful information for teachers and students. *Intervention in School and Clinic, 37*, 156–162.

Chappuis, S., & Chappuis, J. (2008). The best value in formative assessment. *Educational Leadership, 65*(4), 14–18.

Childre, A., Sands, J. R., & Tanner Pope, S. (2009). Backward design: Targeting depth of understanding for all learners. *Teaching Exceptional Children, 41*(5), 6–14.

Clapper, A. T., Morse, A. B., Thurlow, M. L., & Thompson, S. J. (2006). *How to develop state guidelines for access assistants: Scribes, readers, and sign language interpreters.* Minneapolis: University of Minnesota, National Center on Educational Outcomes.

Cohen, A. S., Gregg, N., & Deng, M. (2005). The role of extended time and item content on a high-stakes mathematics test. *Learning Disabilities Research and Practice, 20*, 225–233.

Cohen, L. G., & Spenciner, L. J. (2007). *Assessment of children and youth with special needs* (3rd ed.). Boston: Allyn & Bacon.

Conderman, G., & Koroghlanian, C. (2002). Writing test questions like a pro. *Intervention in School and Clinic, 42,* 34–39.

Cote, D. (2007). Problem-based learning software for students with disabilities. *Intervention in School and Clinic, 43,* 29–37.

Countryman, L. L., & Schroeder, M. (1996). When students lead parent-teacher conferences. *Educational Leadership, 63*(2), 42–47.

Cox, M. L., Herner, J. G., Demczyk, M. J., & Nieberding, J. J. (2006). Provision of testing accommodations for students with disabilities on statewide assessments: Statistical links with participation and discipline rates. *Remedial and Special Education, 27,* 346–354.

Cullen, J., Richards, S. B., & Frank, C. L. (2008). Using software to enhance the writing skills of students with special needs. *Journal of Special Education Technology, 23*(2), 33–43.

Cummings, T. M. (2007). Virtual reality as assistive technology. *Journal of Special Education Technology, 22*(2), 55–58.

Curry, C. (2003). Universal design accessibility for all learners. *Educational Leadership, 61*(2), 55–60.

Davis, A. P., & McGrail, E. (2009). The joy of blogging. *Educational Leadership, 66*(6), 74–77.

Dell, A. G., Newton, D., & Petroff, J. (2008). *Assistive technology in the classroom: Enhancing the school experiences of students with disabilities.* Columbus, OH: Merrill/Prentice Hall.

Dolan, R. P., Hall, T. E., Banerjee, M., Chun, S., & Strangman, N. (2005). Applying principles of universal design to test delivery: The effect of computer-based read-aloud on test performance of high school students with learning disabilities. *Journal of Technology, Learning, and Assessment, 3*(7). Available from http://www.jtla.org

Doyle, M. B., & Giangreco, M. F. (2009). Making presentation software accessible to high school students with intellectual disabilities. *Teaching Exceptional Children, 41*(3), 24–31.

Edgemon, E. A., Jablonski, B. R., & Lloyd, J. W. (2006). Large-scale assessments: A teacher's guide to making decisions about accommodations. *Teaching Exceptional Children, 38*(3), 6–11.

Educational Testing Service (2005). *Reducing test anxiety.* Princeton, NJ: Author.

Edyburn, D. L. (2003). Technology in special education. In M. D. Roblyer (Ed.), *Integrating educational technology into teaching* (3rd ed., pp. 315–333). Upper Saddle River, NJ: Merrill/Prentice Hall.

Edyburn, D., & Basham, J. (2008). Collecting and coding observational data. *Journal of Special Education Technology, 23*(2), 56–60.

Elbaum, B. (2007). Effects of an oral testing accommodation on the mathematics performance of secondary students with and without learning disabilities. *Journal of Special Education, 40,* 218–229.

Elliott, J. L., & Thurlow, M. L. (2006). *Improving test performance of students with disabilities . . . on district and state assessments* (2nd ed.). Thousand Oaks, CA: Corwin.

Elliott, S. N., Kratochwill, T. R., & Schulte, T. R. (1998). The assessment accommodation checklist. *Teaching Exceptional Children, 31*(2), 10–14.

Elliott, S. N., & Marquart, A. (2004). Extended time as a testing accommodation: Its effects and perceived consequences. *Exceptional Children, 70,* 349–367.

Fisher, D., & Frey, N. (2008). Releasing responsibility. *Educational Leadership, 66*(3), 32–37.

Fitzgerald, M. (2008, January 27). The coming wave of gadgets that listen and obey. *New York Times,* p. BU4.

Foegen, A. (2008). Progress monitoring in middle school mathematics: Options and issues. *Remedial and Special Education, 29*(4), 195–207.

Fuchs, D., & Fuchs, L. S. (2005). Responsiveness-to-intervention: A blueprint for practitioners, policymakers, and parents. *Teaching Exceptional Children, 38*(1), 57–59.

Fuchs, L. S., & Fuchs, D. (2001). Helping teachers formulate sound test accommodation decisions for students with learning disabilities. *Learning Disabilities Research & Practice, 16,* 174–181.

Gajria, M., Giek, K., Hemrick, M., & Salend, S. J. (1992, April). *Teacher acceptability of testing modifications for mainstreamed students.* Paper presented at the meeting of the Council for Exceptional Children, Baltimore, MD.

Garcia, S. B., & Ortiz, A. A. (2006). Preventing disproportionate representation: Culturally and linguistically responsive prereferral interventions. *Teaching Exceptional Children, 38*(4), 64–67.

Gee, J. P., & Levine, M. H. (2009). Welcome to our virtual worlds. *Educational Leadership, 66*(6), 48–52.

Geller, L. K. (2005, April). *Universal design for assessments: Including all students in general education assessments.* Presentation at the international meeting of the Council for Exceptional Children, Baltimore, MD.

Glenn, R. E. (2004). Teach kids test-taking tactics. *Teaching for Excellence, 24,* 1–2.

Glor-Sheib, S., & Telthorster, H. (2006). Activate your student IEP team member using technology: How electronic portfolios can bring the student voice to life! *Teaching Exceptional Children Plus, 2*(3) Article 1. Retrieved December 10, 2007, from http://escholarship.bc.edu/education/tecplus/vol2/iss3/art1

Hansen, E. G., & Mislevy, R. J. (2006). Accessibility of computer-based testing for individuals with disabilities and English language learners within a validity framework. In M. Hricko & S. L. Howell (Eds.), *Online assessment and measurement: Foundations and challenges* (pp. 214–261). Hershey, PA: Information Sciences.

Hasselbring, T. S., & Bausch, M. E. (2006). Assistive technologies for reading. *Educational Leadership, 63*(4), 72–75.

Herrera, S. G., Murry, K. G., & Cabral, R. M. (2007). *Assessment accommodations for classroom teachers of culturally and linguistically diverse students.* Boston: Allyn & Bacon.

Hessler, T., & Konrad, M. (2008). Using curriculum-based measurement to drive IEPs and instruction in written expression. *Teaching Exceptional Children, 41*(2), 28–37.

Hetzroni, O. E., & Shrieber, B. (2004). Word processing as an assistive technology tool for enhancing the academic outcomes of students with writing disabilities in the general classroom. *Journal of Learning Disabilities, 37*, 144–154.

Higgins, E. L., & Raskind, M. H. (2005). The compensatory effectiveness of the Quicktionary Reading Pen II on the reading comprehension of students with learning disabilities. *Journal of Special Education Technology, 20*(1), 31–37.

Hoffman, B., Hartley, K., & Boone, R. (2005). Reaching accessibility: Guidelines for creating and refining digital learning materials. *Intervention in School and Clinic, 40*, 171–176.

Hogan, T. P. (2007). *Educational assessment: A practical introduction.* Hoboken, NJ: John Wiley & Sons.

Holzer, M. F., Madaus, J. W., Bray, M. A., & Kehle, T. J. (2009). The test-taking strategy intervention for college students with learning disabilities. *Learning Disabilities Research and Practice, 24*, 44–56.

Hoover, J. (2009). *RTI assessment essentials for struggling learners.* Thousand Oaks, CA: Corwin.

Hopkins, J. (2006). All students being equal. *Technology and Learning, 26*(10), 26–28.

Horn, C., Schuster, J. W., & Collins, B. C. (2006). Use of response cards to teach telling time to students with moderate and severe disabilities. *Education and Training in Developmental Disabilities, 41*(4), 382–391.

Hughes, C. A., Schumaker, J. B., & Deshler, D. D. (2005). *The essay test-taking strategy.* Lawrence, KS: Edge Enterprises.

Hughes, C. A., Schumaker, J. B., Deshler, D. D., & Mercer, C. D. (2002). *Learning strategies curriculum: The test-taking strategy* (6th ed.). Lawrence, KS: Edge Enterprise.

Jones, E. (2008). They can hear you know. *Technology and Learning, 28*(11), 43–46.

Kalyanpur, M., & Kirmani, M. H. (2005). Diversity and technology: Classroom implications for the digital divide. *Journal of Special Education Technology, 20*(4), 9–18.

Kaylor, M. (2008). Use digital storytelling to improve your students' writing skills. *CEC Today,* Retrieved December 16, 2008, from http://www.cec.sped.org/AM/ PrinterTemplate.cfm? Section=CEC_Today1&TEMPLATE

Ketterlin-Geller, L. R., Alonzo, J., Braun-Monegan, J., & Tindal, G. (2007). Recommendations for accommodations: Implications of (in)consistency. *Remedial and Special Education, 28*, 194–206.

Ketterlin-Geller, L. R., Yovanoff, P., & Tindal, G. (2007). Developing a new paradigm for conducting research on accommodations in mathematics testing. *Exceptional Children, 73*, 331–347.

King-Sears, K. E., & Evmenova, A. S. (2007). Premises, principles, and processes for integrating TECHnology into instruction. *Teaching Exceptional Children, 40*(1), 6–14.

Kirby, J. R., Silvestri, R., Allingham, B. H., Parrila, R., & La Fave, C. B. (2008). Learning strategies and study approaches of postsecondary students with dyslexia. *Journal of Learning Disabilities, 41*(1), 85–96.

Knobel, M. & Wilber, D. (2009). Let's talk 2.0. *Educational Leadership, 66*(6), 20–24.

Kozen, A. A., Murray, R. K., & Windell, I. (2006). Increasing all students' chance to achieve: Using and adapting anticipation guides with middle school learners. *Intervention in School and Clinic, 41*, 195–200.

Kretlow, A. G., Lo, Y., White, R. B., & Jordan, L. (2008). Teaching test-taking strategies to improve the academic achievement of students with mild mental disabilities. *Education and Training in Developmental Disabilities, 43*(3), 397–408.

Kurtts, S. A., Matthews, C. E., & Smallwood, T. (2009). (Dis)solving the differences: A physical science lesson using universal design. *Intervention in School and Clinic, 44*(3), 151–159.

Lacava, P. G., Golan, O., Baron-Cohen, S., & Myles, B. S. (2007). Using assistive technology to teach emotion recognition to students with Asperger syndrome: A pilot study. *Remedial and Special Education, 28*, 174–181.

Lambert, M. A., & Nowacek, J. (2006). Help high school students improve their study skills. *Intervention in School and Clinic, 41*, 241–243.

Lancaster, P. E., Lancaster, S. C., Schumaker, J. B., & Deshler, D. D. (2006). The efficacy of an interactive hypermedial program for teaching a test-taking strategy to students with high-incidence disabilities. *Journal of Special Education Technology, 21*(2), 17–30.

Layton, C. A., & Lock, R. H. (2008). *Assessing students with special needs to produce quality outcomes.* Columbus, OH: Merrill/Prentice Hall.

Lenz, B. K. (2006). Creating school-wide conditions for high-quality learning strategy classroom instruction. *Intervention in School and Clinic, 41,* 261–266.

Lenz, K., Graner, P., & Adams, G. (2003). Learning expressways: Building academic relationships to improve learning. *Teaching Exceptional Children, 35*(3), 70–73.

Levine, M. (2003). Celebrating diverse minds. *Educational Leadership, 61*(2), 12–18.

Lindstrom, J. H. (2007). Determining appropriate accommodations for postsecondary students with reading and written expression disorders. *Learning Disabilities Research and Practice, 22*(4), 229–236.

MacArthur, C. A. (2009). Reflections on research on writing and technology for struggling writers. *Learning Disabilities Research and Practice 24,* 81–92.

MacArthur, C. A., & Cavalier, A. R. (2004). Dictation and speech recognition technology as test accommodations. *Exceptional Children, 71,* 43–58.

Maheady, L., Michielli-Pendl, J., Mallette, B., & Harper, G. (2002). A collaborative research project to improve the academic performance of a diverse sixth grade science class. *Teacher Education and Special Education, 25,* 55–70.

March, T. (2006). The new WWW: Whatever, whenever, wherever. *Educational Leadership, 63*(4), 14–19.

McGuire, J. M., Scott, S. S., & Shaw, S. F. (2006). Universal design and its applications in educational environments. *Remedial and Special Education, 27,* 166–175.

McLoughlin, J. A., & Lewis, R. B. (2008). *Assessing students with special needs* (7th ed.). Upper Saddle River, NJ: Merrill/Prentice Hall.

Mellard, D. F., & Johnson, E. (2007). *RTI: A practitioner's guide to implementing response to intervention.* Thousand Oaks, CA: Corwin.

Meltzer, L., Roditi, B., Stein, J., Krishnan, K., & Sales Pollica, M. A. (2008). *Effective study and test-taking strategies for kids with learning difficulties.* Retrieved June 19, 2008, from http://www.greatschools.net/cgi-bin/showarticle/1160

Michaelson, L., & Sweet, M. (2008). Team-based learning. *NEA Higher Education Advocate, 25*(6), 5–8.

Mind Tools (2008). *Memory improvement techniques.* Retrieved June 19, 2008, from http://www.mindtools.com/memory.html

Mitchem, K., Kight, J., Fitzgerald, G., Koury, K., & Boonseng, T. (2007). Electronic performance support systems: An assistive technology tool for secondary students with mild disabilities. *Journal of Special Education Technology, 22*(2), 1–14.

Moats, L. C. (2006, Winter). How spelling supports reading and why it is more regular and predictable than you may think. *American Educator, 12–22,* 42–43.

Montague, M. (2006). Self-regulation strategies for better math performance in middle school. In M. Montague & A. K. Jitendra (Eds.), *Teaching mathematics to middle school students with learning difficulties* (pp. 89–107). New York: Guilford.

Moore Howard, R., & Davies, L. J. (2009). Plagiarism in the Internet age. *Educational Leadership, 66*(6), 64–67.

Mounce, A. B. (2008). Teaching content with interactive whiteboards. *Journal of Special Education Technology, 23*(1), 54–58.

Mustacchi, J. (2009). R U safe? *Educational Leadership, 66*(6), 78–82.

National Board of Medical Examiners (2002). *Constructing written test questions for basic and clinical sciences* (3rd ed.). Philadelphia: Author. Retrieved March 22, 2008, from http://www.nbme.org/PDF/ItemWriting_2003/2003IWGwhole.pdf

Neal, J. D., & Ehlert, D. (2006). 20 ways to . . . Add technology for students with disabilities to the library or media center. *Intervention in School and Clinic, 42,* 119–123.

November, A. (2008). *Web literacy for educators.* Thousand Oaks, CA: Corwin.

Okolo, C. M., Englert, C. S., Bouck, E. C., & Heutsche, A. M. (2007). Web-based history learning environments: Helping all students learn and like history. *Intervention in School and Clinic, 43,* 1–11.

Overton, T. (2009). *Assessing learners with special needs: An applied approach* (6th ed.). Columbus, OH: Merrill/Prentice Hall.

Parette, H. P., Peterson-Karlan, G. R., Wojcik, B. W., & Bardi, N. (2007). Monitor that progress! Data trends for assistive technology decision making. *Teaching Exceptional Children, 40*(1), 22–29.

Parette, H. P., Wojcik, B. W., Peterson-Karlan, G., & Hourcade, J. J. (2005). Assistive technology for students with mild disabilities: What's cool and what's not. *Education and Training in Developmental Disabilities, 40,* 320–331.

Perner, D. E. (2007). No Child Left Behind: Issues of assessing students with the most significant cognitive disabilities. *Education and Training in Developmental Disabilities, 42,* 243–251.

Pike, K., & Salend, S. J. (1995). Authentic assessment strategies. *Teaching exceptional children, 28*(1), 15–20.

Pogue, D. (2008, August 7). Speak up, a computer is listening. *New York Times*, pp. BU1, BU8.

Pomplun, M. (1996). Cooperative groups: Alternate assessment for students with disabilities? *Journal of Special Education, 30*(1), 1–17.

Popham, W. (2006). Those [fill-in-the-blank] tests. *Educational Leadership, 62*(5), 84–85.

Prensky, M. (2008). Turning on the lights. *Educational Leadership, 65*(6), 40–45.

Price, K. M., & Nelson, K. L. (2007). *Planning effective instruction: Diversity responsive methods and management* (3rd ed.). Belmont, CA: Thomson/Wadsworth.

Rao, K., Dowrick, P. W., Yuen, J. W. L., & Boisvert, P. C. (2009). Writing in a multimedia environment: Pilot outcomes for high school students in special education. *Journal of Special Education Technology, 24*(1), 39–49.

Reetz, L. J. (1995, April). *Portfolio assessment in inclusion settings: A shared responsibility*. Presentation at the annual meeting of the Council for Exceptional Children, Indianapolis, IN.

Richardson, W. (2006). The educator's guide to the read/write web. *Educational Leadership, 63*(4), 24–27.

Rozalski, M. E. (2007). Practice, practice, practice: How to improve students' study skills. *Beyond Behavior, 17*(1), 17–23.

Saavedra, S. (2008). Reviewing for a test could be just a click away on your iPod. *San Diego Union-Tribune*. Retrieved March 3, 2008, from http://www.signonsandiego.com/news/education/20080304-9999-1n4ipods.html

Salend, S. J. (2008). *Creating inclusive classrooms: Effective and reflective practices* (6th ed.). Columbus, OH: Merrill/Prentice Hall.

Salend, S. J. (2009). Using technology to create and administer accessible tests. *Teaching Exceptional Children, 41*(3), 40–51.

Salend, S. J., & Garrick Duhaney, L. M. (2002). Grading students in inclusive settings. *Teaching Exceptional Children, 34*(3), 8–15.

Savage, T. V., Savage, K., & Armstrong, D. G. (2006). *Teaching in the secondary school* (6th ed.). Upper Saddle River, NJ: Merrill/Prentice Hall.

Sayeski, K. L. (2008). Virtual manipulatives as an assistive technology support for students with high-incidence disabilities. *Journal of Special Education Technology, 23*(1), 47–53.

Schleibaum, (2007). Using community based social stories to enhance instruction for high school students with moderate disabilities. *Journal of Special Education Technology, 22*(2), 59–64.

Schweder, W., & Wissick, C. A. (2007). Blogging in and out of the classroom. *Journal of Special Education Technology, 22*(4), 63–69.

Schweder, W., & Wissick, C. A. (2009). The power of wikis. *Journal of Special Education Technology, 24*(1), 57–60.

Sedensky, M. (May 2005). *Computers grade student writing*. Retrieved December 8, 2008, from http://www.livescience.com/technology/ap_050509_grading.html

Shaffer, D. W. (2007). Epistemic games as career preparatory experiences for students with disabilities. *Journal of Special Education Technology, 22*(3), 57–68.

Silver-Pacuilla, H., & Fleischman, S. (2006). Technology to help struggling students. *Educational Leadership, 63*(5), 84–85.

Skouge, J. R., Kelly, M., Roberts, K. D., Leake, D. W., & Stodden, R. A. (2007). Technologies for self-determination for youth with developmental disabilities. *Education and Training in Developmental Disabilities, 42*, 475–482.

Skylar, A. A. (2007). Section 508: Web accessibility for people with disabilities. *Journal of Special Education Technology, 22*(4), 57–62.

Skylar, A. A., Higgins, K., & Boone, R. (2007). Strategies for adapting WebQuests for students with learning disabilities. *Intervention in School and Clinic, 43*, 20–28.

Smedley, T. M., & Higgins, K. (2005). Virtual technology: Bringing the world into the special education classroom. *Intervention in School and Clinic, 41*, 114–119.

Songlee, D., Miller, S. P., Tincani, M., Sileo, N. M., & Perkins, P. G. (2008). Effects of test-taking strategy instruction on high-functioning adolescents with autism spectrum disorders. *Focus on Autism and Other Developmental Disabilities, 23*(4), 217–228.

Sopko, K. M. (2008). *Universal design for learning: Implementation in six local education agencies*. Alexandria, VA: National Association of State Directors of Special Education.

Sperling, R. A. (2006). Assessing reading materials for students who are learning disabled. *Intervention in School and Clinic, 41*, 138–143.

Spinelli, C. G. (2006). *Classroom assessment for students in special and general education* (2nd ed.). Columbus, OH: Merrill/Prentice Hall.

Sprankle, B. (2008). Action: Caught on video. *Technology and Learning, 28*(9), 29–32.

Stanford, P., & Reeves, S. (2005). Assessment that drives instruction. *Teaching Exceptional Children, 37*(4), 18–22.

Stern, J., & Avigliano, J. (2008, November). *Differentiated team teaching.* Presentation at the State University of New York at New Paltz.

Stock, S. E., Davies, D. K., & Wehmeyer, M. L. (2004). Internet-based multimedia tests and surveys for individuals with intellectual disabilities. *Journal of Special Education Technology, 19*(4), 43–47.

Strichart, S. S., & Mangrum, C. T. (2010). *Study skills for learning disabled and struggling students* (4th ed.). Saddle River, NJ: Merrill/Pearson Education.

Strobel, W., Arthanat, S., Fossa, J., Mistrett, S., & Brace, J. (2006). *The industry profile on education technology: Learning disabilities technologies and markets.* Retrieved September 5, 2007, from http://cosmos.buffalo.edu/t2rerc/pubs/ip/ET/index.htm

Stromer, R., Kimball, W., Kinney, E. M., & Taylor, B. A. (2006). Activity schedules, computer technology, and teaching children with autism spectrum disorders. *Focus on Autism and Other Developmental Disabilities, 21,* 14–24.

Tam, K. Y., & Heng, M. A. (2005). A case involving culturally and linguistically diverse parents in prereferral intervention. *Intervention in School and Clinic, 40,* 222–230.

Tennessee Department of Education. (2008). *"Test-time" strategies for students, parents, and teachers.* Retrieved December 14, 2008, from http://www.tennessee.gov/education/assessment/doc/tsteststrategies.pdf

Terrill, M. C., Scruggs, T. E., & Mastropieri, M. A. (2004). SAT vocabulary instruction for high school students with learning disabilities. *Intervention in School and Clinic, 39,* 288–294.

Test-taking tips for parents. (2008). Retrieved July 8, 2008, from http://www.testtakingtips.com/parents/index.htm

Therrien, W. J., Hughes, C., Kapelski, C., & Mokhtari, K. (2009). Effectiveness of a test-taking strategy on achievement in essay tests for students with learning disabilities. *Journal of Learning Disabilities, 42*(1), 14–23.

Thompson, J. R., Bakken, J. P., Fulk, B. M., & Peterson-Karlan, G. (2005). *Using technology to improve the literacy skills of students with disabilities.* Naperville, IL: Learning Point Associates.

Thompson, J. R., Meadan, H., Fansler, K. W., Alber, S. B., & Balogh, P. A. (2007). Family assessment portfolios: A new way to jumpstart family/school collaboration. *Teaching Exceptional Children, 39*(6), 19–25.

Thompson, S. J., Johnstone, C. J., & Thurlow, M. L. (2002). *Universal design applied to large scale assessments (Synthesis Report 44).* Minneapolis: University of Minnesota, National Center on Educational Outcomes.

Thompson, S. J., Quenemoen, R. F., & Thurlow, M. L. (2006). Factors to consider in the design of inclusive online assessments. In M. Hricko & S. L. Howell (Eds.), *Online assessment and measurement: Foundations and challenges* (pp. 102–117). Hershey, PA: Information Sciences Publishing.

Tomlinson, C. A. (2008). Learning to love assessment. *Educational Leadership, 65*(4), 8–13.

Towles-Reeves, E., Kleinert, A., & Muhomba, M. (2009). Alternate assessment: Have we learned anything new? *Exceptional Children, 75*(2), 233–252.

Villano, M. (2006). Classroom management software. *Technology and Learning, 26*(10), 8–12.

Walker, C., & Schmidt, E. (2004). *Smart tests: Teacher-made tests that help students learn.* Portland, ME: Stenhouse Publishers.

Wang, L. (2005). The advantages of using technology in second language education. *THE: Technological Horizons in Education, 32*(10), 38–42.

Weinstein, C. E., Palmer, D. R., & Schulte, A. C. (2002). *LASSI user's manual* (2nd ed.). Clearwater, FL: H & H Publishing.

Whittaker, C. R., Salend, S. J., & Duhaney, D. (2001). Creating instructional rubrics for inclusive classrooms. *Teaching Exceptional Children, 34*(2), 8–13.

Williams, B. (2007). *Educator's podcast guide.* Washington, DC: International Society for Technology in Education.

Willingham, D. T. (2009). What will improve a student's memory? *American Educator, 32*(4), 17–25.

Wissick, C. A. (2005). Written language: When to consider technology. *Technology in Action, 1*(6), 1–12.

Yell, M. L., Busch, T. W., & Rogers, D. C. (2007). Providing instruction and monitoring student performance. *Beyond Behavior, 17*(1), 31–38.

Yell, M. L., Katsiyannas, A., & Shriner, J. G. (2006). The No Child Left Behind Act, adequate yearly progress, and student with disabilities. *Teaching Exceptional Children, 38*(4), 32–39.

Yell, M. L., & Rozalski, M. E. (2008). Academic interventions: Effective instruction. In M. Yell, N. Meadows, E. Drasgow, & J. Shriner (Eds.), *Educating students with emotional and behavioral disorders in general and special education classrooms* (pp. 282–335). Upper Saddle River, NJ: Merrill/Prentice Hall.

Zorfass, J. M., Fideler, E. F., Clay, K., & Brann, A. (2007). Enhancing content literacy: Software tools help struggling students. *Technology in Action, 2*(6), 1–12.

Index

CORWIN
A SAGE Company

The Corwin logo—a raven striding across an open book—represents the union of courage and learning. Corwin is committed to improving education for all learners by publishing books and other professional development resources for those serving the field of PreK–12 education. By providing practical, hands-on materials, Corwin continues to carry out the promise of its motto: **"Helping Educators Do Their Work Better."**